BOSTON CELTICS
WHERE HAVE YOU GONE?

ROBERT PARISH, NATE ARCHIBALD, BILL SHARMAN, AND OTHER CELTIC GREATS

MIKE CAREY
AND MICHAEL D. McCLELLAN

SPORTS PUBLISHING

Sports Publishing books may be purchased in bulk at special discounts for sales promotion, corporate gifts, fund-raising, or educational purposes. Special editions can also be created to specifications. For details, contact the Special Sales Department, Sports Publishing, 307 West 36th Street, 11th Floor, New York, NY 10018 or sportspubbooks@skyhorsepublishing.com.

Sports Publishing® is a registered trademark of Skyhorse Publishing, Inc.®, a Delaware corporation.

Visit our website at www.sportspubbooks.com.

10 9 8 7 6 5 4 3 2 1

Library of Congress Cataloging-in-Publication Data is available on file.

ISBN: 978-1-61321-062-8

Printed in the United States of America

To former Celtics team physician Arnold Scheller and his family.
A Special Forces medical officer, Dr. Scheller served in the Gulf War,
Iran, Kosovo, Somalia, and the Balkans. In recognition of his valor,
he was awarded the Bronze Star for "his critical high-risk missions
to disrupt Al-Qaeda and Taliban operations and for his role as
a member of the Joint Services #12 and #121 in support of
Operation Enduring Freedom."

Also, to Chief Warrant Officer 5 David Nolan, who has been a
maintenance test pilot for helicopters for 25 years. During his
distinguished military career, he has served a year in El Salvador, a year
in Korea, ten months in Kuwait, 27 months in Iraq, a year in Egypt,
and 28 months in Afghanistan.
—Mike Carey

✤✤✤

To the memory of my father, Jack D. McClellan. I love you, Pops.
—Michael McClellan

CONTENTS

Where Have You Gone?

M. L. CARR

Positive Influence

Some people choose to see the glass half full, regardless of the adversity or circumstance. They are born to lead, to inspire, to motivate. They carry the rest of us across the finish line when we've long since given up on the race. They're dreamers. They make the impossible possible, and, to quote the late Sir Winston Churchill, they see the opportunity in every difficulty.

Spend any time at all with former Boston Celtics player/coach/general manager Michael Leon Carr and it's hard not to pick up on that type of positive vibe, the kind that makes you feel reinvigorated and ready to take on the world. Maybe it's because M. L. Carr has spent his entire life overcoming, proving the doubters wrong, and reaching heights that others would have thought unimaginable.

It's a circuitous route to success, one that started at tiny Guilford College in Greensboro, North Carolina, and continued with a fifth round selection in the 1973 NBA Draft. Picked by the Kansas City Kings, Carr also found himself selected by the Kentucky Colonels of the now defunct American Basketball Association. For a good-but-not-great player aspiring to a career in professional basketball, the future did indeed look bright. However, the eternal optimist from Wallace, North Carolina, quickly learned that the path wouldn't be easy.

"I spent three years trying to figure out how to get into the NBA or the ABA," Carr says from his corporate office in Huntsville, Alabama. "I was cut from three teams, including the Kings and the Colonels, and I ended up playing that season in the old Eastern League. Then I was contacted by Red Auerbach of the Boston Celtics, who wanted to hide me for a year. He saw something in me, so he asked me to go overseas to play basketball. And that's what I did. I packed my bags and went to Israel, where I played for a team called the Israel Sabras."

Carr's play in Israel helped him to grow as a player, and in the process get noticed by basketball executives in the States. Carr led the Sabras to the league title, topping the league in scoring and finishing second in rebounding en route to being named Most Valuable Player. Flush with options, Carr decided to sign a one-year contract with the Spirits of St. Louis in the ABA.

"St. Louis was a great learning experience for me," Carr says. "I played with a great group of players, but we weren't a great team. We didn't play together. It was one of the greatest teams ever from a talent standpoint—a young Moses Malone was on that team. Caldwell Jones. Marvin Barnes. Don Chaney. Mike D'Antoni. It was a great team, talent-wise, but we just didn't put it together that year. There was a lot of turmoil. Our head coach was Rod Thorn, but by the end of that year the coach was Joe Mullaney."

Carr's brief career in the ABA yielded season averages of 12 points and 6 rebounds, earning him a spot on the league's All-Rookie team. The NBA took notice—specifically, the Detroit Pistons of the NBA. The courtship was fast and furious, and Carr wasted little time signing his first NBA contract. He would play three seasons in a Detroit uniform, two of those for Herb Brown and one for Dick Vitale. Unfortunately for Carr, the Pistons had future Hall-of-Fame center Bob Lanier but not much else. While the Pistons were anything but one of the league's elite, Carr enjoyed his time in Detroit and has nothing but fond memories of a certain coach-turned-announcer.

"Dick was a very animated coach," Carr says. "It was his first pro coaching job. He'd come over from the University of Detroit, and he was just like he is now as an announcer—intense. There's one thing I'll always thank Dick for—he allowed me to play the third most minutes in the league that year, which was my free agent year. That helped me achieve my dream of becoming a high-paid athlete."

That big contract, of course, came courtesy of the Boston Celtics. Auerbach, true to his word, continued to keep tabs on the swingman who had led Guilford College to a small college national championship. He saw Carr as a key piece in a rebuilding puzzle, and the Celtics had plenty of rebuilding to do. Boston had won two NBA Championships during the 1970s, with John Havlicek and Dave Cowens serving as the cornerstones of those titles. With Havlicek retired and Cowens breaking down, the Celtics were coming off a 29-win season, and also one of the most tumultuous in team history. Fortunately for Boston fans everywhere, Auerbach had gambled on a certain junior-eligible from French Lick, Indiana, and the wait for Larry Bird was finally over.

"When I got there, Dave Cowens was making every effort to be a part of the rebuilding process. Tiny Archibald was coming back from an off year. Gerald Henderson was there. Cedric Maxwell. And then we had this young kid from French Lick who was coming in and was supposed to be a heck of a player.

"So there was a lot of optimism at that time. There had been a lot of turmoil the year before, and there were decisions made to overhaul the team and to get rid of all the guys that were causing all of the problems. Red wanted good players but he didn't want to sacrifice character in the process. So as we put that thing back together, we had a very good year.

We didn't win it, but we came very, very close. And for me, it was a dream-come-true because Pete Maravich played on that team and he was my childhood idol."

The Celtics would finish 61-21 that season, losing to rival Philadelphia in the 1980 Eastern Conference Finals. It was a learning experience, and one that would set the stage for a rematch with the 76ers the following season. Down 3-1 in the 1981 Eastern Conference Finals, the Celtics rallied to take the epic series 4-3 and advance to the 1981 NBA Finals against the Houston Rockets.

"Red just kept telling us to focus on one game at a time," Carr says, recalling the dramatic comeback against the Sixers. "Those last three games were all nail-biters, but we just stayed focused and did what we had to do. We knew we had the talent—we had Larry, we had Robert Parish and Kevin McHale. We had Nate Archibald. Cedric Maxwell. So we just went out there and took care of business.

"I remember getting fouled by Dr. J [Julius Erving] late in Game 5 and going to the line. I needed to hit those free throws or the season was over. The Sixers called timeout to try and ice me, and I remember Cedric Maxwell coming over to me and telling me to relax. He told me that if I hit the shots that we'd play on in the next game, and that if I missed them we'd start our vacation early.

"It was an incredible comeback. And we knew when we took that series that we were going to win the NBA Championship. The NBA Finals was anticlimactic in that respect, because we'd just beaten the team we felt posed the biggest obstacle."

And just like that, Carr was on top of the basketball world.

"As a Celtics fan growing up, and knowing the mystique of the franchise, it was the greatest feeling in the world to win that championship," he says. "After being cut from all those teams and having to play in Israel, it was such a rewarding experience to finally be recognized as the best. I'll never forget it. And the fact of the matter is, we knew that we were going to beat the Houston Rockets. We knew they couldn't hurt us. We were the best team in the league and we just had to go out there and do it. There's not another feeling in the world like winning a championship.

"I remember coming back from Houston, and going through the airport. The fans were unbelievable. They were going absolutely crazy. I'd never witnessed anything like that. And then that parade and seeing all of those fans—it was surreal because I'm a history major and I knew what had happened just three years earlier in Boston. It was the height of busing in the city, and I vividly remember the young black man being poked with the American flag, the racial tensions in the neighborhoods, and all of that was resonating with me as we traveled that parade route and saw all of those fans cheering us. Cheering me! I mean, here I am traveling the parade route as a hero, as a black athlete, and all of these fans celebrating our accomplishment on the basketball court. And I remember thinking at the time how great it would be to bottle this. Today Boston is one of the greatest cities in the world. I like to think our championship played a small part in putting those dark days behind it."

The Celtics would win another championship in 1984 with Carr on the roster, defeating the hated Lakers in seven games. It was a classic, one of the greatest ever played—Bird versus Magic, blue collar versus Showtime, East Coast/West Coast. It remains one of the highest rated NBA Finals in league history.

"Our motto that year was 'Don't Be Denied,'" Carr says. "More than anything, what stands out now was the last seconds of that final game. No one believed we could beat the Lakers. No one. They were the thoroughbreds and we were the Clydesdales. It was a very physical series. McHale's hit on Rambis, Bird knocking Michael Cooper backwards, so many memories. We knew we had to physically beat them up. You had Jack Nicholson giving us the choke sign. East Coast-West Coast. It was a series that truly captured the world's attention. Being in the Boston Garden with twelve seconds left on the clock, there's nothing like it. I get chills today just thinking about it."

And did Carr's positive attitude help influence that series?

"I feel that I played a major role from the standpoint of motivating players, telling them that we needed to seize the moment. Using the towel as a motivator. Taking the heat off the other Celtics players—there were times when I would take the pressure off the guys because I brought a bravado that antagonized a lot of the opposing players. I think that helped take the heat off of Larry, Robert and Kevin.

"My attitude the whole time was that we expected to win. That was my message during the series, and that was what I told anyone who would listen afterward. So I think I had an effect and I think I contributed to that championship. I remember going to LA after that series was over and walking into a restaurant—and the waiter wouldn't serve me. He told me he wouldn't serve me because I waved my white towel and got under his skin. I told him that was great, because I didn't want his greasy burger anyway."

Carr's NBA career would end at the end of the 1984-'85 playoffs, but his work with the Celtics wasn't done. He remained connected with the team, and in 1994 was named general manager. He also coached the Celtics for two seasons—1995-'96, and 1996-'97. It was a dark period in team history—Bird, McHale, and Parish were long gone, and the team had lost budding star Reggie Lewis to a heart attack during the summer of '93. Still, Carr worked hard to restore glory to the once-proud franchise as GM.

"I got that opportunity because I was trying to purchase the team from Paul Gaston," Carr says. "Paul didn't have an interest in selling at that time, so he approached me about running the team. He said that anyone who was chasing him as hard as I was in terms of trying to buy the team could definitely work for him running it.

"It was a great experience because it gave me an opportunity to give back to the fans who had been so good to me through the years, and it gave me a chance to help the Celtics through a tough time. The talent just wasn't there. Eventually I decided to coach the team because I felt it would help me better assess the personnel on the roster. Red Auerbach tried to talk me out of it because he felt that I was going to take some hits. The franchise was really down, and it was on a downward trend. The best coach in the world can't win if the talent isn't there. But the plan was to coach long enough to get some building blocks in place and then hand it over to someone else. It was a tough job, but I wouldn't trade the experience for anything. I truly enjoyed it."

Today, Carr's focus has moved to the business world, where he is the President and COO of The Dream Company, LLC, which focuses primarily in the insurance arena. The Dream Company provides risk management solutions in the life, disability, and long-term care markets.

"We are an insurance marketing firm," Carr says proudly. "What we've been able to do is take an online delivery system that we've built in-house and allow institutions to use it—non-profit organizations, colleges, religious organizations, multi-level marketing firms—and allow them to sell a term-life product as a fund-raiser for those institutions. In other words, you buy a policy and you are able to donate a portion of that to your affinity group. For example, in my case that affinity group could be Guilford College. It's a very innovative product, and one that has to potential to raise an enormous amount of money for those types of institutions."

While Carr may find himself in the corporate world now, his heart will always be with the Celtics. He stays connected to many of his former teammates, including Bird, and he catches the games on TV. He admires what Danny Ainge has done with the team, and is convinced that Ainge has what it takes to rebuild the Celtics once again.

"Danny's a very bright guy," Carr says quickly. "He knows what he's doing, and he has the right attitude when it comes to running a team. It's important to stay positive and focused on the ultimate goal, even when everyone else around you might be calling for your head."

Where Have You Gone?

FRED ROBERTS

Staying Power

FRED ROBERTS

**College: Brigham Young | Height: 6'10' | Weight: 227 lbs.
DOB: 08/14/1960 | Years with Celtics: 1986-'87 through 1987-'88
Position: Forward**

Notes: Selected 27th overall in the 1982 NBA Draft by the Milwaukee Bucks. Teammates with both Larry Bird and Magic Johnson.

The sports world has always been a star-driven universe, the imaginations of its fans fueled by extraordinary performances under pressure: Joe Montana's precision passing in the Super Bowl, David Beckham's creative shot-making in the World Cup, Albert Pujols's towering home runs in the World Series. The stars sell the tickets and the jerseys, and they drive television revenue through the ceiling in the process. Larry and Magic arrived when fan interest in professional basketball was at an all-time low; their battles sparked the NBA's Golden Age, and the league transformed itself into a global marketing machine thanks in large part to their epic rivalry. And the same can be said for individual sports—in golf there has always been an Arnold Palmer, or a Jack Nicklaus, or a Tiger Woods, their larger-than-life personas filling the galleries and attracting the sponsors. Imagine tennis without the historic achievements of players like McEnroe, Sampras, Agassi, Nadal, or Federer. Would we even care about the Tour de France without Lance Armstrong?

But sports cannot exist on stars alone. For every Wayne Gretzky there are hundreds of grinders doing their best to make a roster, to make a contribution, to make a living doing what they love to do the most. You see them every time you turn on the TV to watch your favorite team. You cheer for them make a big play, or sometimes just to see them get into the game. Some of them flash briefly across the sky, only to get cut or injured and disappear from view forever. But others have staying power. These are the athletes that have both the talent and the luck to persevere, and they know their place in the sports universe. They do their jobs and are always ready when called upon, and they forge a successful career as a professional athlete.

Fred Roberts is such a man. Roberts played his college basketball at Brigham Young University during the late '70s and early '80s, and even at the collegiate level he could be described as anything but a star. That mantle went to teammate Danny Ainge, who would be named college basketball's player of the year as a senior. But Roberts was long and athletic and could run the court, and he worked hard to improve his game. He played in 119 games for the Cougars, averaging 15.5 points and seven rebounds while shooting 54.6 percent from the field. His contributions helped to spark a basketball renaissance at BYU, and in the process he garnered the attention of NBA scouts, with the Milwaukee Bucks taking him in the second round of the 1982 NBA Draft.

"I was motivated to go to Brigham Young," Roberts says. "My older brother played on the basketball team, and I had hoped to play with him. Danny was a year ahead of me. He came in and brought a new excitement to the school and to the basketball program. We had a good time. My junior year—Danny's senior year—we had that run to the Elite 8. We beat UCLA and beat Notre Dame before losing to Virginia. That Notre Dame game was the game where Danny sprinted the length of the court and scored on Kelly Tripucka to win it at the buzzer. So I had a great time playing ball at BYU."

Roberts chose to play basketball in Europe rather than jump directly into the NBA, a decision that would, ironically, add years to his career on the back end; it was while playing in Italy that Roberts realized the value of being in top physical shape and being able to run the floor, something he was able to do for parts of 13 NBA seasons.

"My best year in college was my junior year," Roberts says. "My senior season was a disappointment. Danny was gone, which meant that we were bringing in a pair of freshmen guards. And I don't think I was ever in as good a shape as I needed to be at that level. As a result, I was drafted a lot deeper than I thought I would be.

"Don Nelson was the Milwaukee coach at the time, and he made it sound like I was going to have a real hard time making the team. So I went overseas, which was good in some ways because we worked really hard. I was always a pretty good runner, but I'd never had a coach who really pushed his players as hard as my coach in Italy. And when I came back, I was a big man who could run, which really served me well. I think that's the reason I was able to stay in the league as long as I did."

While in Italy, Roberts was traded from the Bucks to the New Jersey Nets, who, in turn, would trade him to the San Antonio Spurs. The latter transaction was also notable in that it involved a head coach—Stan Albeck—one of the few times in the league history that a coach was a part of a trade between teams.

"I joke about it," Roberts says, laughing. "I like to tell people that I've been traded for everything but a player!"

And how, exactly, did Roberts end up in a trade involving a coach?

"When I was in Italy, an NBA team came over and played some exhibition games. Stan Albeck was the coach of that team, and he was in San Antonio at the time. They played us, and I really excelled that night. I scored 43 points and really played well, and I think Albeck may have gone back to San Antonio and told some people to keep me on their radar. And as luck would have it, I'm property of the Nets, and Albeck later decides he wants to coach in New Jersey. So my rights were included as compensation for Albeck being allowed to leave San Antonio to coach the Nets."

Roberts returned to the U.S. following one season in Italy, joining the Spurs for the 1983-'84 regular season. This San Antonio team featured the likes of George Gervin, Artis Gilmore and John Lucas, and finished with a 37-45 record, narrowly missing the playoffs. The next season, Roberts found himself traded after playing 22 games for the Spurs, landing on a Utah Jazz team coached by Frank Layden and led by a rookie point guard named John Stockton. And although the Jazz finished with a 41-41 record, Roberts found himself in the NBA Playoffs for the first time in his career. The Jazz upset the favored Houston Rockets 3-2, winning twice in Houston to advance to the Western Conference Semifinals. Despite losing to the Nuggets, 4-1, the playoff experience was truly special for the forward from Provo, Utah.

Karl Malone would join the Jazz via the 1985 NBA Draft, and it soon became clear that he was going to be a star. Roberts's minutes and scoring average both took a hit, and his future with the team became cloudy. The NBA Champion Boston Celtics were in the market for a player to solidify their front line, and in September of 1986 they offered Roberts a two-year deal to join the team. Utah matched the offer, eventually trading Roberts to Boston for a future draft choice. This transaction was also notable, because included in the trade was an agreement for the Celtics to play an exhibition game in Utah. With the Celtics one of the biggest road draws in the league, and with the team featuring Larry Bird in his prime, having the Celtics come to Salt Lake City was a financial boon to the city and the team.

Had highly touted draft pick Len Bias not died from a cocaine overdose the previous June, Roberts's arrival in Boston probably wouldn't have happened at all. But the Bias tragedy created the need for a forward to provide spot relief for Larry Bird and Kevin McHale. The 1986-'87 Boston Celtics remain, in the minds of many, one the most resilient teams in NBA history; battling through injuries to key players such as Bird, McHale, Robert Parish, and Bill Walton, the Celtics slugged their way through the Eastern Conference before eventually falling to a deep, healthy, and rested Los Angeles Lakers squad. That playoff run was filled with memorable moments, including

Bird's steal of Isiah Thomas's inbounds pass to save Game 5 of the Eastern Conference Finals. And through it all there was Roberts, the consummate professional, doing his part to help the Celtics succeed.

"With Boston losing Bias, the Celtics needed to pick up another big guy and that's how I ended up on the team. And, boy, was I nervous. These guys had just won the world championship. And every time they'd come to San Antonio or Utah they'd whipped up on us. In fact, that last season in Utah, Bird came out and had a quadruple double. So I knew what kind of team I was joining. It was hard for me to get completely comfortable, but I hung in there and tried to do my best to help the team. We fought through so many injuries that year—Walton, McHale, Parish—and that playoff run was like a war. We just didn't have enough to get it done.

"For some reason I always felt that there were two teams within that team, at least from the public and the media point-of-view: There was the five starters, and then there was the rest of us. I always felt that if we won, it was the starters who were responsible. If we lost, then it was the bench who let them down. That was kind of a hard thing for me, and a challenge mentally. But it was still a great experience. Seeing those warriors go toe-to-toe against the Pistons in the playoffs—guys were playing injured, guys were getting mugged by players like Bill Laimbeer, Rick Mahorn, and Dennis Rodman. My respect for them just went through the roof."

What was it like playing with the Big Three?

"Unbelievable," Roberts says. "I'll never forget speaking to Robert for the first time. In public he never really said much, but that first day he just walks up and slaps me on the back and says 'What's up?' He was completely different than what I had pictured in my mind. And he was such a great, great teammate.

"Larry was just unbelievable. He was one of those guys who just thrived on the challenge, a guy who always rose to the occasion. He really invited that challenge to be put on him. He wanted it as tough as possible, and he liked to prove that he could rise above it and come out on top.

"Kevin played that Pistons series on one leg—I still don't know how he managed to ignore the pain. He just refused to give in, and he played his heart out."

By the end of the 1987-'88 regular season it was clear that the Celtics were a team in transition. Boston left Roberts unprotected during the '88 NBA Expansion Draft, and the Miami Heat immediately took him. In another twist of fate, Roberts was immediately traded to the Milwaukee Bucks, the team that had drafted him in the first place. And, ironically, Roberts would play five seasons with the Bucks—the longest stretch with one team in his career—while also enjoying his best statistical seasons.

There would be three more NBA stops for Roberts—Cleveland (1994-'95), Los Angeles (1995-'96), and Dallas (1996-'97), with a stint in Spain and the Continental Basketball Association sandwiched in between. Exactly what you would expect from a pro's pro, the kind of player who grew up loving the game of basketball and who worked hard to forge a long and successful career playing with—and against—some of the greatest stars the game has ever known.

Today, Roberts is a grade school teacher at Lincoln Academy in Pleasant Grove, Utah.

"When I finished my career I kept my house in Milwaukee," Roberts says. "But our family lived in Utah, so we eventually made the decision to move back home. I kind of fell into education—for five years I served as a principal at a private school. That gave me a chance to transition into something that I really enjoyed, which is working children and their families. I went back to school and got my degree in education and my teaching certificate. That was in 2007, and that's when I started teaching sixth grade."

What was it like leaving the game of basketball?

"It was a difficult transition," he says quickly. "I didn't think it was going to be as difficult as it was. I just loved the game of basketball—everything about it. I loved the competition, I loved the camaraderie of being on a team. It was a great life—playing a great gym every night, getting to play against great players, so I really missed that a lot. So I was looking for something to fill that void, and that's when I found education. I think because I'm able to work with children that it gives me some of that excitement and joy of seeing success, and seeing people struggle and having success. It puts life back into my life."

Roberts, it turns out, hasn't completely left the game of basketball behind. He's also the basketball coach at Lincoln Academy.

"It may not sound like much," Roberts says with a laugh, "especially when Danny Ainge is the president of the Boston Celtics and I'm coaching a junior high team, but it doesn't matter what level you're competing at. Being involved in sports is one of the greatest things you can do in your life, and I really enjoy working with these kids at Lincoln Academy. I wouldn't want to be doing anything else."

Where Have You Gone?

WALTER McCARTY

Mr. Versatile

Today's NBA landscape is dotted with versatile big men, the kind of players who can score both inside and out, the kind of players who can box out and battle for the big rebound on one possession, and who can also step behind the three-point line and knock down a trey on the next. Dirk Nowitzki is the prototype, but there are others—think Kevin Durant and Lamar Odom and you get the point.

Walter McCarty is such a player, and for parts of eight NBA seasons McCarty brought that versatility to the Boston Celtics, his blue collar game on display for a city that prides itself on hard work for an honest day's pay. The fans loved McCarty, and still do to this day. The 6'10" forward could run the floor with the best of the NBA's bigs, in part because that was the style of basketball he played for Rick Pitino while at the University of Kentucky. He could drain a three in transition, or he could fight for rebounding position underneath the basket. It was a skill-set that helped the Wildcats win the 1996 NCAA Basketball Championship and helped keep McCarty employed by the NBA for a decade. Not bad for a player who came to the game relatively late; McCarty, who grew up in Evansville, Indiana, didn't start playing organized basketball until he was eleven.

"I shot ball every now and then," McCarty says, "but I didn't play on a team or in a league until I was in the fifth grade. Most of my friends and classmates did—they were either coached by their parents, or playing in some kind of league, whether it was at the YMCA or in a church league, but that wasn't me. I was just tall and out there in the neighborhood playing with the other kids. And when I did start playing ball in school, the biggest jump for me was from eighth grade to my freshman year at Harrison High School. That's when I realized I could really become a good basketball player if I put in the work, and that motivated me to keep working and improving my game. Before you know it, I was headed to Kentucky."

Living on the Kentucky-Indiana border in Evansville, Indiana, McCarty and his family were fans of the Kentucky basketball program. Indiana University recruited McCarty, as well as McCarty's good friend Calbert Cheaney, but McCarty didn't feel that the bruising Big 10 fit his game. So while Cheaney headed off to Bloomington, McCarty opted for the SEC and a Wildcat program on the rise under head coach Rick Pitino.

"I pretty much knew I wanted to play for Kentucky," McCarty says. "Playing on those AAU teams, I got close with guys like Tony Delk and Jared Prickett, and that was a big factor in my decision. Plus, I was really attracted to the style of ball that Rick Pitino had implemented."

The decision turned out to be fortuitous for McCarty. By his senior season, the Wildcats were loaded with future NBA players such as McCarty, Delk, Derek Anderson, Ron Mercer, Antoine Walker, Nazr Mohammed, Wayne Turner, and Mark Pope. The team finished the season 34-2, capping it all with a 76-67 win over Syracuse for the national championship.

"Kentucky fans are the greatest fans in the world," McCarty says, smiling. "It was a privilege to play there, and those were some of the best years of my life. The journey to the championship was incredible. We knew we were talented and had the potential to be great, but what we had went much farther than just talent. We were such a close team. We really enjoyed each other's company and hanging out with each other away from the basketball court. We truly cared for each other, and those relationships stand to this day."

McCarty was selected by the New York Knicks with the 19th pick in the '96 NBA Draft. For McCarty, while the draft experience was the culmination of years of hard work, it was also the realization of a dream-come-true.

"It was the greatest feeling ever," he says. "To be able to do things for your family that you never thought you'd be able to do, that's just the greatest feeling in the world. I'd always dreamed of buying my parents a new house, and giving them a new car, but you don't think you'll ever be in that position. And then suddenly you're able to help them and take some of that pressure off of them.

"And I never took it for granted. I knew that I had to prove myself, and that I had to go out there every day and show the coaches that I belonged in the NBA. I also knew that I had to earn my salary, and fortunately I had the work ethic to go out there and do the things to perform in this league. It was a challenge, no question about it, and in many ways it was about starting over again. I had to go out there and earn my minutes and earn my respect, just like when I was a freshman at Kentucky."

Unfortunately, McCarty joined a veteran Knicks team, and minutes would be hard to come by. The team was coached by Jeff Van Gundy, and was loaded with talented players like Patrick Ewing, Allan Houston, Larry Johnson, John Starks, Charles Oakley, and Buck Williams. Playing time, especially that first season, was going to be hard to find.

"It was great for me, though. I was the year that I learned the most about being a professional basketball player. People always ask me how I could learn so much when I didn't play much, and I tell them all of those guys you just mentioned were great mentors. Collectively, they took me under their wing and showed me what it was to be a professional. Things like staying prepared, taking care of my body, getting the proper amount of rest. How to do the right things in practice. How to watch film. All of those things."

McCarty took those things with him the following season, when he arrived in Boston and found himself reunited with Walker and Mercer. Pitino, hired away from Kentucky and facing the formidable task of rebuilding the Celtics, knew that McCarty would bring the energy needed to help duplicate the success enjoyed in Lexington. At least that was the plan at the time.

"Coach P needed guys who knew his system," McCarty says. "And what better guys than us three? We'd just previously played for him at the college level, and he knew that we would be in the kind of shape that he needed.

"I remember how the trade went down—I was getting ready to play in the last preseason game before the start of the 1997-'98 NBA regular season; the Knicks were literally hours away from playing the Celtics in that game, and I get a call in my room telling me that I've been traded to the Celtics. So I knew that I wouldn't be playing that night. A Celtics coach picks me up, and I go to the game as a guest of the Celtics.

"It was the highlight of my career, being traded to the Celtics. That team has so much history, and there have been so many great players to have played there. And all of those championships . . . it was just a great place to play."

On the surface it looked like Pitino would be the Celtics savior. However, there were problems almost from the start. At Kentucky, Pitino played a high-pressure game, something that wasn't ideally suited for the pros.

"It was tough," McCarty says. "Coach P was able to turn Kentucky around, but the Celtics situation was a lot different. You're dealing with a salary cap, a longer schedule, the mindset of the professional athlete. And then there was the style of ball that he wanted to play. He wanted the up-tempo style, the high-pressure style, but I just don't think that can work for an 82-game schedule. There were a lot of games that it worked for us, and then certain times when it didn't. I think if he could have taken the reins off a little bit he could have been a helluva NBA coach.

"At Kentucky he was adored, in the pros I think he found out that it was truly a business. It's a different type of pressure. It was hard to find the guys who would buy into his system at that level, and it ultimately wore on him mentally. I think that's what led him to walk away in frustration. I think he realized that he was best suited for the college game."

While Pitino was headed back to college, it was Jim O'Brien who stepped in, first on an interim basis and then helping lead the Celtics back to the playoffs following the 2001-'02 season. For McCarty, reaching the playoffs was another dream-come-true.

"We were ready. We just knew we were going to get after it defensively that season. We took it upon ourselves to keep opponents from scoring on us—our goal was to contest every shot and force our opponents into low field goal percentages. We really started to trust the system and to trust one another. We trusted that if a guy got by one of us, that someone would be there to play help defense. It was a great experience for us, because we came within two games of reaching the NBA Finals."

While the playoff run meant so much to McCarty, he quickly learned what resurrection of the Celtics meant to the old guard.

"I've been so lucky, privileged, and blessed," McCarty says. "To get to know people like Bob Cousy, Bill Russell, and Tom Heinsohn, I could never truly put into words what these people mean to me. And as much as I love Tom Heinsohn—he's a very special person in my life—his late wife Helen was one of the most special people I've ever known. God bless her—she passed away from cancer, and it was one of the hardest things for me to deal with emotionally. She was such a special lady, and meant so much to me and my family. I love her dearly."

McCarty would play 44 games for the Celtics during the 2004-'05 season before being traded to the Phoenix Suns for a conditional draft pick. He would retire a season later, after playing 36 games for the Los Angeles Clippers. To this day he remains a Celtic at heart.

"That's the place that I call home. The fans are the best in the world. They know their basketball and they appreciate blue collar players who play hard and know their role. That was me. I tried to do my best to help the team win—if that meant diving for loose balls or running to my spot and shooting a three, I could tell that the fans really appreciated the things that I did while wearing a Boston Celtics uniform."

Today, McCarty is an aspiring singer-songwriter. His new R&B CD, titled *Emotionally,* is the result of his lifelong passion for music.

"When I was four or five, I was singing with my family in the church. And as I got older, I started singing in middle school choir, then high school and church choir, and on the street corners with my friends. When I went to Kentucky, I selected the School of Fine Arts.

"I've always loved music. In 2003 I released my first CD, *Moment for Love,* but I really didn't have the time I needed to promote it due to playing basketball. I have a recording studio in my home, and about a year ago I had the urge to express myself musically, so I started writing again and decided it was time to put out another CD. It's been great, because now I have the time to promote it. I recently performed the title track at halftime of a Miami Heat-Chicago Bulls basketball game. So I'm doing what I love and having a great time."

Does McCarty regret not winning a championship with the Celtics?

"Absolutely not," he says. "Would it have been special? There's no question, I would have loved to have won an NBA Championship. That's what we all dream about as players. But I was fortunate to win an NCAA championship at Kentucky, and I was able to play 10 years in the NBA, many of those with the greatest franchise in professional basketball. I feel like I'm part of a special family in that regard. And I'm not someone who is defined strictly by what he did on the basketball court. I have other interests, like my music and my family, and I'm content with how my life has played out to this point. It's been great, and I'm looking forward to the future."

Where Have You Gone?

GREG KITE

Walking Tall

GREG KITE

College: Brigham Young | Height: 6'11" | Weight: 250 lbs.
DOB: 08/05/1961 | Years with Celtics: 1983-'84 through
1987-'88 | Position: Center

Notes: Two-time NBA Champion as a player with the Boston Celtics (1984, 1986).

There is an old saying in basketball, its originator lost to the ages, but one suspects it came moments after the legendary Wilt Chamberlain first walked on a basketball floor for Overbrook High in Philadelphia as a 7-foot freshman.

"You can't coach size," the saying goes, and it has yet to be disproved.

Coaches can teach you how to shoot, how to play defense, how to dribble, and how to pass. They can teach you the zone defense and the dribble-drive offense.

They can't teach you to be 6'11", and they can't teach you to possess the raw-boned strength that makes it nearly impossible to back down such a force of nature in the low post. Such is the case with Greg Kite, a

250-pound backup center for the Boston Celtics during the NBA's Golden Age of the 1980s.

Kite, born and raised in Houston, was seemingly destined for the NBA from a young age. Always taller than most kids in his class, Kite had grown to be 6'10" by the time he was 15, at which point he gave up other sports to focus exclusively on basketball.

"I was playing in the baseball all-star game," Kite said, "and when I struck out three times chasing curve balls, I realized baseball wasn't my game. So that was the end of that. I learned later that the pitcher went on to become a pretty good pitcher for Texas A&M, so it wasn't like I was getting smoked by a bad pitcher."

By his senior year at Madison High School, Kite was being recruited by many of the premiere hoops programs in the country. Duke wanted him. Kentucky and UCLA also were chasing him. Family connections to BYU led him to Provo, where he joined a program on the rise, with hotshot junior guard Danny Ainge leading the way.

"We went to the NCAA Tournament during my first two years there," Kite says. "Danny's senior year—my sophomore year—we went the deepest, making it all the way to the Elite 8 before losing to Ralph Sampson and the Virginia Cavaliers. The game before that, Danny had that famous full-court dash to the basket against Notre Dame, dribbling past Kelly Tripucka and John Paxson, and putting in that scoop layup around Orlando Woolridge for the win. It's still one of the most memorable plays in college basketball history."

As fate would have it, Kite would later join Ainge in Boston, a late first round draft selection by legendary patriarch Red Auerbach. The year was 1983, and the Celtics were loaded with All-Stars in search of their second NBA championship in the '80s. Larry Bird, Kevin McHale, and Robert Parish were all in their prime, and their focus was on beating the best teams in the East before the inevitable collision with the vaunted Lakers in the NBA Finals. They knew it wouldn't be easy; Milwaukee was loaded with talent, and the Philadelphia 76ers were the reigning world champions.

Into this environment stepped Kite, the bruising rookie from Brigham Young. During his summers he'd played against some of the best college talent in the country, not to mention some of the bigger names in the NBA. So while the sight of the Big Three was certainly impressive, Kite was not in awe. He arrived at that first training camp determined to earn a spot on the team, and to do whatever he could to help the Celtics achieve their goal.

Says Kite: "I'd been playing basketball a long time by the time I made it to that first training camp, so in a lot of ways I wasn't star-struck by playing for the Celtics or playing with the guys that I'd seen on TV so often. But every now and then I'd catch myself just thinking about these guys, and how big they were to fans all over the world. It was in those quiet moments that it usually hit me the hardest."

Kite's role was limited that first season, and his contributions often went unseen and unrecognized by the public. His size and strength were felt by the starters during competitive scrimmages, internal wars that only increased in intensity when Bill Walton joined the team two seasons later. And Kite also kept himself ready to play when called upon—no easy feat when your minutes are limited and sporadic at best, and you're not a part of the normal eight-man rotation.

"The biggest adjustment as a rookie is the long season," says Kite. "You're used to the long practices as a rookie, because most college practices are equally long. But there are just so many more games in the NBA. And I think it's actually harder on rookies who aren't playing a lot. If you're not playing much, it can get to be a little bit tedious, because you've got to be patient and keep yourself ready. You've got to continue to work hard. You don't have a lot of live practice time. That's something that I did as rookie—I worked hard to keep myself in shape, and I stayed after practice for extra work and things like that. It was something I continued to do throughout my entire NBA career."

The Celtics fired on all cylinders during Kite's rookie year. The team had added Dennis Johnson via trade during the off-season, with the Phoenix Suns' asking price coming in the form of center Rick Robey. For the Celtics, the addition of DJ proved to be brilliant. Johnson brought lock-down defense and clutch shooting to the back-court, something that had been missing the previous two seasons. It also created an opening for a big man, and Auerbach didn't hesitate to select Kite late in the first round of the draft.

"The Rick Robey for Dennis Johnson trade opened up a spot for a backup center," Kite says. "Red Auerbach really wanted to pick Roy Hinson from Rutgers. Hinson was a heck of a player who ended up having some knee problems later on, and Roy had really long arms like Kevin McHale. He could reach four or five inches higher than I could, even though he was only 6-foot-9. So Red had been hoping he would last until the Celtics could pick, but Roy was selected by Cleveland. I was the alternative. Red knew who I was—BYU played St. John's and St. Joe's in a holiday tournament at Madison Square Garden in New York, and Red had been there scouting. I didn't think much about it then, but I must have made an impression on him."

To call Kite's rookie year a dream-come-true would be an understatement. He was a member of the greatest franchise in NBA history, and the Celtics would win regular season and playoff games in bunches. The 1984 NBA Finals brought together the league's two most storied teams, and its two most marketable personalities. It was Celtics versus Lakers, East versus West. And, more than anything else, it was Bird versus Magic. This confluence of events is widely recognized as the launch point for the most successful period in league history.

And Kite, while he may not have played a large role in the outcome, certainly had one of the best seats to witness history in the making.

"I remember M. L. Carr telling me to enjoy the ride," Kite says, smiling, "because not all rookies end up playing in the Finals and having a chance to win a championship. And that was very true. He had been in the league a long time and had never been close to winning a championship. And then, when he makes it to the Celtics his dream is realized. But he was quick to point out that it doesn't always work out for everyone. In my case, I was fortunate to be in the NBA Finals four years in a row, I definitely appreciated being around some of the greatest players in history, and being a part of that great series against the Lakers."

So many moments in '84: Gerald Henderson's steal, which saved the series for the Celtics. Bird, calling his team out after a humiliating loss in

Los Angeles. Kevin McHale, with his clothesline of Kurt Rambis in the next game. DJ's huge shot with the clock running down to level the series and send it back to Boston 2-2. Cedric Maxwell's bold Game 7 proclamation that the Celtics 'get on my back,' and then backing it up with an awesome performance to help seal the team's 15th NBA Championship.

"It was a great experience," Kite says. "Everything about it. Having that great rivalry with the Lakers and meeting them in the Finals, that was big for everyone at that time. And playing against those great teams in Philly and Milwaukee just to get there, that was tough as well. It was a great basketball atmosphere, and it was great to be a part of it."

For Kite, the next three seasons in Boston would end with annual trips to the NBA Finals—two painful losses to the Lakers with a victory over Houston sandwiched in between. And in each of those seasons Kite continued to work hard and make his mark as the consummate professional, always ready when called upon, always eager to help the team win. For those who saw those great Celtics-Lakers battles, who can forget how Kite frustrated the legendary Kareem Abdul-Jabbar with his physical style of defense during the NBA Finals?

Kite would eventually find himself waived by the Celtics in February of '88, which led to an eight-year odyssey with the Los Angeles Clippers, Charlotte Hornets, Sacramento Kings, Orlando Magic, New York Knicks, and Indiana Pacers. It was a journeyman's life to be sure, and Kite would never again taste the NBA Finals, but this second act in his career also afforded him the opportunity to grow as a player and explore the boundaries of his athletic gifts.

"The Clippers experience was good for me," Kite says. "It was the exact opposite of the Celtics in that it was chaos as an organization, and it was a team that wasn't winning and didn't have a winning tradition. But it was good for me from the standpoint that I actually got to play significant minutes for the first time in my career. Same thing with Sacramento. So those next two-and-a-half years were good for me in terms of getting to play. I got to go out there and make mistakes and get minutes on the court. That really helped establish me in the league as a backup who could come in and help a team in an eight or nine-man rotation.

"From there I signed a one-year contract with Orlando, which was great because it's where my wife was from. We met at BYU, where she played basketball on the women's team. It was great to be able to come home there, because we had a young family. I ended up getting a four-year deal and ended up there. I was very thankful for the opportunity. That first year I started all 82 games. Orlando was a second year expansion team, and that's the year we had Scott Skiles and Sam Vincent on the team. The next year is when they selected Shaquille O'Neal, so I got to back up Shaq for a year and a half. That's when I hurt my Achilles tendon, which was the only serious injury I ever had, so I had to sit out the rest of that year.

"Orlando added Penny Hardaway, and I ended up being released by the Magic. I played briefly for the Knicks and then ended up with the Pacers. That's the year the Magic made it to the NBA Finals, beating us in the Eastern Conference Finals to get there. So it was a good experience there.

"From BYU to the pros, it was a fun experience all the way around. I was lucky to marry a wonderful woman in college, play for two Celtics championship teams, and then play for the Magic those years because it was so close to home. We have 10 children, and their ages range from 10 to 26 years old. Two sets of twins. My wife said she wanted a big family, so I think we covered that pretty well."

Today, Kite resides in Orlando with his family and is involved in the real estate and mortgage industries. He has his real estate, securities, and insurance licenses, and is currently doing independent work in all of these areas. He's also devoting time to a new network marketing opportunity, which is doing very well. He and his wife, Jenny, also own and operate a private school. It's a nonprofit enterprise with very little income derived from it, but it's something the family really enjoys.

"It's a labor of love," Kite says proudly. "It's something that we continue to do as a family."

Life for this former Celtic has turned out very good indeed.

Where Have You Gone?

JEFF JUDKINS

He'd Play for Free

JEFF JUDKINS

College: Utah | Height: 6'6" | Weight: 185 lbs. | DOB: 03/23/1956
Position: Guard | Years with Celtics: '78-'80

Notes: Second-round draft choice (30th pick overall) by the Celtics in 1978, the same year Boston selected Larry Bird with the sixth overall pick. Selected by the Dallas Mavericks in the 1980 expansion draft.

Quiet but confident, 6'6" rookie swingman Jeff Judkins, the second-round draft choice of the Celtics in 1978, seemed destined to have a long and productive career ahead of him in Boston. As a clutch outside shooter who averaged better than 18 points a game during his college career, he had led the University of Utah to two NCAA berths. In the Celtics' training camp, his play was so impressive that by opening day of the regular season, he had earned a spot in Coach Tom "Satch" Sanders's regular rotation rather than learning the pro game by observing from a seat at the end of the bench.

Playing almost 19 minutes a game, he shot better than 50 percent from the field, averaging 8.8 points, 2.4 rebounds and a steal per game. By far, he was Boston's most consistent and enthusiastic reserve. "I was thrilled to be a part of the Celtics' tradition," Judkins says. "It was just so exciting—even at practice—for a 22-year-old kid like me to be playing with such great players as Dave Cowens, Nate Archibald, and Cedric Maxwell. And, like everyone else on the team, I was very much aware that Larry Bird, who had been drafted by Boston with the sixth overall pick of the '78 draft but chose to remain at Indiana State for his final year, would be joining the club the following season."

Under new head coach Bill Fitch, though, Judkins's minutes decreased in 1979-'80 because Boston had added versatile rookie guard Gerald Henderson and defensive stopper M. L. Carr to its roster. However, the competitive youngster made the most of the ten minutes of playing time he averaged. For the second straight year, he shot 50 percent while also hitting 82 percent of his free throw attempts.

"We ended up with a 61-21 record and made it to the Eastern Conference finals before the Philadelphia 76ers knocked us out, 4-1," he says. "It was such a fun season that I was 100 percent sure I wanted to spend my entire career with Boston. I was going to be a free agent, so late in the season I walked into General Manager Red Auerbach's office and sat down with him and Coach Fitch. I wanted to make certain management knew I had no plans to sign anywhere else but with Boston. I looked Red right in the eyes and told him, 'This is the only place I want to be. If you sign me to another contract, I don't care what salary I get. You can write any dollar figure you want on the contract and I'll sign it without even looking at what I'll be making. We can do it right now. That's how much I want to be part of this team.' Auerbach and Fitch looked at me as if I was absolutely out of my mind. I mean players just don't tell their teams they don't care about what they'll be making."

Auerbach, impressed by the second-year player's attitude, told Judkins he'd discuss his contract situation as soon as the season ended. Unfortunately, for the 23-year-old, there was an expansion draft to be held in late May to stock the NBA's newest team, the Dallas Mavericks, with a full roster of players. Boston decided to leave 32-year-old "Pistol Pete" Maravich and Judkins unprotected. The Mavs, seeking to build its franchise with young, promising talent, selected the always hustling kid who loved being a Celtic.

"I knew Dallas was going to take me," Judkins says. "Pete wasn't happy in Boston and was ready to retire and almost everyone Dallas was choosing was under 25."

In his brief stay with the Celtics, Judkins, who was All-State in football, basketball, and baseball at Highland High School in Salt Lake City, developed a close friendship with Bird. "As everyone knows, Larry was so tough, so strong, and so fearless every minute he was on the court," Judkins says, "but I saw a different side of him when he came out to Utah and visited me. My family had a houseboat on Lake Powell and we'd go cliff diving once or twice a week. My buddies and I would dive off cliffs which were 20 to 30 feet above the water. Larry, he chickened out every time. "I ain't gonna kill myself," he'd tell us. "This isn't my sport."

So, we found smaller cliffs, maybe eight feet above the lake. He still wouldn't dive in. He'd just sit there drinking a beer or two while all the rest of us were unmercifully kidding him about being more scared than a five-year-old girl.

"The next day, we ran into a little storm while cruising around on the houseboat. An inch or two of water ended up on the deck from the heavy rain. It really wasn't much at all. We look at Larry and he's running to find a life preserver to put on. He's turning white as a ghost, almost in panic mode. We're all giving him grief because he's the guy who supposedly fears nothing. Then he tries to make excuses. 'Hey, I got a ten-year career ahead of me, and I'm not going to just sit here and wait to drown as this leaky piece of junk sinks to the bottom of the lake.' He probably will deny everything about how he was scared to death during a little downpour and about how he was too frightened to dive into the water from a tiny cliff— but it's all true."

Although selected by Dallas, Judkins never played a minute for the expansion team. Upon becoming a free agent on July 1, 1980, he opted to sign with Utah, for whom he would play 62 games during his lone season with the Jazz. "Not to make excuses, but the style of play was entirely different than it had been in Boston," he says. "Guys didn't pass the ball much. They didn't look to find the open guy. My shooting percentage went way down [although he did shoot better than 88 percent from the foul line]. To this day, I feel Boston was the perfect fit for me. I looked at myself as a good team player, someone who just wanted to contribute." But Judkins, despite some serious lobbying by Bird, never made it back to Boston.

He would go on to be a seldom used reserve in Detroit and Portland before retiring after the 1982-'83 season. At age 26, he entered the business world, eventually becoming an executive with Safelite Auto Glass, the nation's leading glass and replacement service company. During the summers, he ran youth basketball camps in the Salt Lake City area.

In 1989, he accepted an offer from University of Utah head coach Rick Majerus to join his staff, with recruiting and scouting as his principal responsibilities. Among some of his prized signings of high school prospects were Keith Van Horn, Andre Miller, Michael Doleac, and Hanno Mottola, all of whom went on to play in the NBA, as well as Trent Whiting, who enjoyed a long and successful overseas career.

Although Majerus had a reputation of being a demanding boss, Judkins terms his 10 years as an assistant coach at his alma mater as one of the greatest learning experiences of his life. "Coach is a great teacher of every aspect of the game," he says. "That's why he's such a consistent winner. But in 2000 when Brigham Young University offered me the chance to become director of basketball operations, along with being an assistant coach on the men's team, I thought it was the right time to move on."

Shortly before his second year at BYU, Judkins accepted the women's head coaching position. It's a job he still holds, setting new records each season. Since taking over the bench duties, BYU has received five NCAA tournament bids, including one appearance in the Sweet Sixteen. In addition, Judkins's teams have earned three trips to the NIT.

Following this past season, Judkins was voted West Coast Conference Coach of the Year, with his squad losing to DePaul, 59-55, in the opening round of the NCAA tournament and finishing the season at 26-7. Judkins also reached another milestone by becoming BYU's all-time winningest women's basketball coach with 231 career victories (versus 115 losses).

Five times during his 12-year tenure, his teams won 20 or more games. Three times they were conference regular season champions. Only once has a Judkins-led team suffered a losing season. "Women's basketball reminds me of how NBA teams played in the '80s. Because they are slower than the men, they can't easily take their defender off the dribble. Instead, they have to rely on defense and offensive teamwork to find ways to get easy baskets. That's how basketball was meant to be played," Judkins declares. "I can't stand to watch NBA basketball or even some men's college games because it's all one-on-one stuff. There's no passing, no cutting off picks, no setting of screens. It's just not my kind of basketball. Plain and simple, it's boring."

Jeff, now 55, and his wife, Mary Kay, reside in the Provo area and have five children and two twin grandchildren, Jocelyn and Judd.

Where Have You Gone?

WAYNE KREKLOW

The Strange Case of the Missing Championship Ring

WAYNE KREKLOW

**College: Drake University | Height: 6'4" | Weight: 175 lbs.
DOB: 1/4/1957 | Position: Guard | Years with Celtics: 1980-'81**

Notes: Originally selected by Celtics in third round of 1979 draft. Cut by Celtics in first year of pro career. Played for Maine Lumberjacks in 1979-'80. Earned roster spot with Celtics for '80-'81 season. Played in 25 games before being waived. Today, he and his wife, Susan, are co-head coaches of the men's and women's volleyball teams at the University of Missouri.

For 30 years, Wayne Kreklow never knew the Celtics had awarded him a championship ring for being a member of the 1981 club that defeated the Houston Rockets, 4-2, in the title series. "I got a phone call last year from a memorabilia collector asking me if I wanted to sell my '81 championship ring," said Kreklow. "I told the guy that I never received a ring because I had been cut halfway through the season."

The Drake University graduate, who was chosen by the Celtics in the third round of the 1979 draft, was cut by Boston in his first year as a pro. Still determined to play in the NBA, Kreklow signed with the Maine Lumberjacks in the CBA, where he averaged 9.6 points.

Celtics head coach Bill Fitch took notice of Kreklow's hustle and work ethic and decided to bring him back for the '80-'81 training camp. Admittedly, the unheralded guard had little or no chance of making the squad, with Nate "Tiny" Archibald, M. L. Carr, Chris Ford, and Gerald Henderson on the 11-man roster. In addition, Kreklow would have to beat out Ronnie Perry Jr. from Holy Cross, a 23-point-a-game college scorer and Boston's third-round pick in 1980.

Despite considerable criticism from many in the media, Fitch chose Kreklow over Perry for the final backcourt spot.

In the team's seventh game of the season, Carr broke the fifth metatarsal in his right foot, which would force him to miss 41 games. Kreklow, instead of being anchored to the bench, was given the opportunity to fill in on occasion, averaging four minutes a game and scoring 1.2 points a game, most of which came in garbage time.

"Just being on the court with guys like Larry Bird, Kevin McHale, Robert Parish, and Tiny Archibald was a huge thrill," Kreklow says. "I just tried to make good passes, play solid defense, and stay out of everybody else's way. I usually shot the ball once, maybe twice a game.

"What I learned during my time with the Celtics was that without good character and integrity, talent only takes a team so far. All the Celtic players were class individuals. It was a near-perfect combination of players from top to bottom."

A few weeks before Carr was fully recovered from his injury, the Celtics signed shooting guard Terry Duerod, who had been waived by the Dallas Mavericks. When Carr was activated, Kreklow was waived. Fitch, in breaking the news to Kreklow, asked the 24-year-old to stay in Boston and practice with the team. "If we get another injury, I'll have you right here to fill the spot," the coach said.

For the rest of the year, Kreklow practiced with the Celtics at home but did not travel. When the playoffs began, Fitch invited Kreklow to join the team on the road even though he was ineligible to play.

After Boston defeated Houston on the road for the title, Kreklow was flattered when he was asked to ride on one of the trucks in the victory parade through Boston. "I thought it was a kind gesture, considering I hadn't played a minute after January."

In September of '81, Kreklow received a call from his parents. They told him the Celtics had sent him a letter inviting him to the ring presentation ceremony. "I had mixed emotions. I was flattered that I'd get asked to be there, but I felt it would be just too awkward to stand off to one side while everyone else received their rings. The thought never crossed my mind that I'd be given a ring because I hadn't been a part of the team for the final four months of the year. In the end, I decided I'd feel too out of place."

Kreklow also realized his days with the Celtics were through. "They had drafted a guard, Charles Bradley of Wyoming, in the first round, and had chosen Danny Ainge, who was under contract with the Toronto Blue Jays, with the 31st pick overall," he says. "I eventually signed a contract to play in Australia, which paid a lot more than the CBA."

For years, the Celtics held on to Kreklow's ring, wondering when he would come and pick it up. That day never came. "No one ever told me I was getting a ring and I honestly didn't expect one," Kreklow says. "For all these years, I knew nothing about the ring. I was just happy to be able to say that I played 25 games for a world championship team."

Kreklow took away many valuable lessons from his year in Boston. "My wife, Susan, and I split the head women's volleyball coaching duties at Columbia College for 10 years, where our teams won two national NAIA championships, going undefeated in both seasons with an 85-0 record. From the start, we modeled our teams after the Celtics, making sure we had quality players on my team. When 'Team Kreklow' moved on to the University of Missouri, we basically shared the coaching duties. Combined, we've gone 222-119 over 11 years."

It's been more than three decades since the Celtics '81 ring ceremony was held. Kreklow's ring, in all probability, is now officially lost or permanently misplaced. "It's still nice to know that the Celtics were so kind to me, so generous," he says. "I look back and know that playing for Boston that year was the greatest sports experience of my life."

Meanwhile, the Celtics, now knowing the true story behind Kreklow's failure to ever pick up his ring, contacted Balfour, the makers of the championship rings, and arranged for a duplicate to be made this year.

"I just want to thank the Celtics, especially [Vice President of Media Relations] Jeff Twiss, for going to great lengths to have the ring made for me. I wear it with a great deal of pride. It's an honor I never expected.

"One of the great moments in my life was watching my three children, Ricky, Ryan, and Ali, as they each tried on my ring."

Where Have You Gone?

MARK ACRES

Class Act

MARK ACRES

**College: Oral Roberts | Height: 6'11" | Weight: 225 lbs.
DOB: 11/15/1962 | Years with Celtics: 1987-'88 through 1988-'89
Position: Center**

Notes: Four-time Honorable Mention All-American (1981-'85). Inducted into the Oral Roberts Athletic Hall of Fame (2003). Played eight seasons in the NBA. Signed by Boston as a free agent on May 7, 1987. Selected from Boston by Orlando in the NBA expansion draft on June 15, 1989.

The students at J. R. Hull Middle School in Torrance, California, all look up to their teachers, but there is one faculty member in particular who stands out above the rest. He's tall, quiet, and unassuming, and once upon a time his height helped make him one of the most highly recruited athletes in the country. These students, who were born more than a decade after he played his last game, are, at most, vaguely aware of his claim to fame. They're tuned into their own digital world, connected by text messages and Twitter feeds, their smartphones filled with the latest music by hip rappers like Lil Wayne and country stars like Taylor Swift. They are all about the New Millennium in all phases of their lives, including the sports they play and the athletes they idolize. They dream of being the next David Beckham or Maria Sharapova, scoring goals and winning major championships while attaining global fame and fortune in the process. And yet in many ways these students are no different from typical adolescents of generations past. They thrill at the thought of meeting players from their favorite teams, of going to ballpark with glove in hand, and of collecting the autographs of stars and role players alike. The difference between the students at J. R. Hull Middle School and most other schools is that the giant of a man who walks among them has competed against the likes of Magic, Michael, and Shaq. He is 6'-11" and not far from his playing weight of 225 pounds, dimensions that came in handy during another career, this as a member of one of the greatest franchises in NBA history.

Meet Mark Acres, man-in-the-middle turned middle school teacher.

"Teaching is very rewarding for me," Acres says of his work at J. R. Hull Middle School, while happily fielding questions about his basketball career. The one-time Boston Celtic may be decidedly 'old school' to students who weren't even born when he played the game, but then Acres doesn't expect them to appreciate what it was like playing with Larry Bird, Kevin McHale, and Robert Parish. "It's a different generation. These kids have their own heroes. They have their favorite players, whether it's a LeBron James or a Kobe Bryant, and they don't really care about players that they haven't seen before."

And while the Big Three may have given way to the Three Rs, Mark Acres is still very much in tune with the NBA and what makes it so popular around the globe.

"I played in Europe for two years," he says, "and even back then you could see the influence that the NBA was having overseas. And then you look at how far the league has come today—you have impact players like Yao Ming from China, who had become an elite center before the foot injury forced him to retire. You have players like Manu Ginobili from Argentina, Dano Gallinari from Italy, and Tony Parker from France. All of them are All-Star caliber players. And look what Dirk Nowitzki has done with his career. He's one of the biggest stars in the game. He has won an NBA Most Valuable Player Award, and he's been the MVP of the NBA Finals. So now more than ever the game has gone global. More people than ever before can identify with the players in the NBA."

Located in Torrance, California, J. R. Hull is the perfect place for Acres to do what he loves most: Impacting the lives of young people. And while his students may only have a passing knowledge of his accomplishments on the hardwood, they certainly appreciate what he does in his current capacity.

"I enjoy teaching," Acres says proudly. "It's something that I've always wanted to do, so I went back to school after retiring from the NBA and completed my masters in education."

Acres's dual loves—teaching and athletics—came from his father, Dick, who was a high school basketball coach and, later, the head coach at Oral Roberts University. Dick Acres stressed the fundamentals of the game, insisting that his son master everything from the outlet pass to the midrange jumper. Mark responded by channeling his prodigious basketball talent. He focused on one sport, becoming a true student of the game, and also one its biggest fans. Growing up in Inglewood only served to fuel the fire.

"I was a Laker fan growing up," he says of a childhood spent in the shadows of West, Baylor, and Chamberlain. "They were always very competitive, and their best battles were always with the Celtics—which made it interesting when I landed in Boston."

Attending Palos Verdes High School, Acres excelled at both athletics and academics. It was very much a Utopian environment, with little in the way of trouble, which left Acres free to hone his basketball skills. He was mobile for a big man, with good footwork and a nice touch around the basket, exactly the types of things that recruiters were looking for in a Division I basketball player. A spot on the McDonald's All-America Team didn't exactly hurt matters.

"It was an honor to be selected," Acres offers modestly. "Being chosen as an All-American puts you in about the top twenty-five players in the country. I'm sure a few are left off that deserve to be there, but those things are beyond your control. So it was a very nice honor, and I still cherish it today. I still have my McDonald's ring, as well as some booklets from the game."

With scholarship offers pouring in, there was little doubt where Acres would end up.

"I followed my father to Oral Roberts. It was a pretty natural transition for me, because he'd been my coach for my whole life. So that part was pretty easy. I was used to his system and to the way he coached. And I knew what he expected from me."

Acres made the college leap look easy, being named to the All-American team following his freshman season. It would become an annual rite of spring; unheard of today, Acres finished his collegiate career by receiving the honor four years running.

"Earning a place on the team was very special to me," says Acres. "To be recognized once is great, but to do it at every stage, from my freshman season to my senior season—that is something I'm very proud of. And if I had to pick one that meant more than the others, I'd have to say my junior season. That was the year that we went to the NCAA Tournament. It was—and still is—only the second time that has happened in school history."

Acres was drafted in the second round of the 1985 NBA Draft by the Dallas Mavericks. With three first-rounders competing for roster spots ahead of him, it didn't take Acres long to realize that he was being squeezed in a time-honored NBA numbers game. He opted to play two seasons in Europe instead, where he could further prepare his game for the premiere league on the planet. It turned out to be a wise decision; rather than waiting to be cut by the Mavs and toiling in the CBA, he was able to join a team that could play him major minutes. Instead of languishing on a bench, he was able to fill a significant role on a European playoff contender. He posted averages of 19.5 points and 10 rebounds his first season overseas, and topped that with 20 and 16 the following year. A polished Acres returned to the States in '87.

"My first year in Europe was not a very pleasant one," Acres concedes. "I was very homesick, and I missed my family, and it just seemed like I was missing a whole lot. But then I got used to it, and knew what to expect, and it became a lot easier the second time around. I really enjoyed it. If I had the time, I'd like to get back to Europe every year."

While living in Europe may have been difficult from an emotional standpoint, there was a huge upside to plying his trade in a foreign land—free agency. Back then this didn't mean an instant avalanche of money, as it does in so many cases today, but at least it meant that Acres could contact other clubs regarding his services. And when the Mavericks selected Roy Tarpley in 1986, they effectively renounced their rights to the big man from Oral Roberts.

Acres returned in '87 a different player—faster, stronger, more confident in his abilities. The Celtics were still reeling from the death of Len Bias, in June of '86, and were trying to prepare for life after Larry, Kevin, and Robert. It was a very well-timed union.

"I liked my chances of making the team," Acres says of his first training camp with the Celtics. "That was one of the reasons I left Dallas to play overseas. I wanted to join a team with an opportunity to play. With the Celtics, that opportunity existed. It was the first time I'd stuck it out and went to all the camps, including veteran camp. It was exciting, but it was also a mental and physical drain. Very demanding. You keep playing, you try to do your best, and you try not to leave anything to chance."

Larry Bird averaged a career-high 29.9 points-per-game during the 1987-'88 season. For Acres, guarding Larry Legend in practice was unlike anything he'd ever experienced in basketball.

"It was always a challenge," he says, laughing. "He was a fantastic scorer, and an even better basketball player. You just tried to get a hand on the ball or deny him the pass. Anything to keep the ball out of his hands."

Injuries to Kevin McHale and Bill Walton opened to door for Acres and fellow rookie Brad Lohaus, and early on the duo made the most of the opportunity. But then, with the playoffs approaching, head coach K. C. Jones shortened his rotation and both players saw their minutes shrink. How could they complain? The Celtics were still a power in the East. And sit as they might, they were still members of the most fabled franchise in basketball, and their teammate was one of the best players to ever set foot on a court. Never was that more apparent than in Game 7 of the 1998 Eastern Conference semifinals. Most people remember it as the famous shootout between Larry Bird and Dominique Wilkins.

Acres remembers it this way: "What an incredible series. We had just beaten the Hawks in Atlanta in Game 6. Larry was talking trash after the game, saying that the Hawks had their chance. He told the press that the Hawks had blown their chance, and that the Celtics were going back to the Boston Garden to close it out.

"So we came back to Boston for that Game 7, and he and Wilkins were just going at it. They were matching each other basket-for-basket, and at the end of the game I asked Larry if that was the best he'd ever played. Larry smiled and just said 'Yep.' I'd never seen anything like it."

After one more season in Boston, Acres was made available for the expansion draft. Orlando quickly snapped him up. He played three seasons in a Magic uniform, before spending parts of the 1992-'93 season in Houston and Washington. Curiously, Acres still has one of the highest three-point percentages in Magic history, going 5-10 for his career and finishing with a .500 percentage from behind the arc.

"I didn't shoot that many, but I made some," Acres says with a laugh. "I don't think I'll make anyone forget about Dirk or Larry."

Still, he considers himself a Boston Celtic. The longtime Laker fan is now a part of the Celtic family, and has nothing but fond memories of his time spent in New England. He appreciates the history of this proud franchise, and remains a big fan of the legendary Red Auerbach.

"Red was a genius," he says, "and such a great teacher. He'd been retired from coaching for more than twenty years by the time I got there, but that didn't stop him from watching the practices and making suggestions on how to do something better. Whether it was boxing out or passing the ball, he would take the time to work with me. The thing I found most interesting was that you could always smell his cigar before you saw him coming [laughs]. The cigar—and all that smoke—are the things I'll never forget about him."

Like Red, Acres can't resist teaching. "I guess I got some of that from my father. I knew I was going to teach from a very early age. I enjoy working with young people and having a chance to impact their lives in a positive way. Some people ask why I didn't follow my father's footsteps into coaching, but I wasn't interested in coaching as a profession. I enjoy conducting basketball camps and working with young athletes in that capacity, so I'm sure I'll always be connected to the game in some way."

And while Acres may not be officially involved in the game he loves, he still plays basketball on a recreational level. From 2002-2009, his team finished the season as the Redondo Beach Men's Open Basketball League Champions.

"Keeps me in shape," Acres says. "We have a lot of fun out there on the court. Great camaraderie, and a good way to remain competitive. We have a good mix of young and old guys. I definitely fall into that latter category [laughs]."

The highlight of Acres's basketball career came on January 29, 2009, when he was inducted into the Oral Roberts University Athletics Hall of Fame.

"It was a great, great honor," he says, smiling. "To be recognized in that way is very special, and something that I'm very proud of and will always cherish."

Whether giving instruction on the court or in the classroom, one thing remains apparent: Mark Acres is in a class by himself.

Where Have You Gone?

JOHN BACH

Born to Be a Coach

When John Bach signed a $5,000 contract to play for the Celtics back in 1948, the Navy veteran who had served in the Navy at Okinawa thought he would spend a year or two in basketball and then "get a real job" in the business world. "But," says the former guard, "the sport never managed to find a way to get rid of me. I've been hanging around for 60 years."

Although still an active and astute assistant coach with the Chicago Bulls, where he was in charge of the team's defensive strategy, Bach made the decision to retire and leave basketball behind after the 2005-2006 season. "This is my last year," he said at the time. "I'm 81, and I think 81 is a nice round number." He had been a coach in the pro ranks for 27 years. Before that, he had spent 28 years as a college head coach. His memories of his brief playing career in Boston have not faded with time.

"You hear basketball people talk about the 'Celtics family.' Well, it was true even when I played for them," the still-spry 87-year-old says. "Boston owner Walter Brown treated everyone so tremendously, so generously. For instance, somehow Mr. Brown found out I was about to get married, so he walked over to me, said congratulations, and handed me five one hundred dollar bills. Totally unexpected, but it was typical of how caring a person he was. Then there was [public relations director] Howie McHugh, who felt it was part of his job to watch over the players and make sure they knew they had him for a friend. If you had a problem, no matter how small or large, Howie was right there to help you solve it. The entire front office always made the players feel as if they were special."

In those days, the team practiced at Boston University, and many of the players, including Bach, lived in a large room just down the corridor from the gym. "It was a Spartan existence. We paid two dollars a night to rent a cot," he recalls. "You'd get up in the morning, have some cereal, walk about 20 steps, and start scrimmaging."

The coach of the '48-'49 Celtics was Alvin "Doggie" Julian, who would go on to coach Dartmouth College for 17 seasons and be elected into the Basketball Hall of Fame.

"Doggie was the type of guy who could scare the hell out of you," says Bach, who was one of only two rookies on the club, the other being guard Tommy Kelly. "He'd really push you to your limits. He always let you know that if you didn't produce, he'd find someone else who could.

"He used to tell us, 'You always have to play hard. You have to love the game. If you don't, you'll find yourself out of basketball, driving a cab somewhere.' Well, a few years later, I was walking down a street in New York and this taxi driver pulls over and starts beeping his horn at me. I look over and it's my old Boston teammate, John Ezersky. First words out of his mouth: 'Tell that SOB Julian that his prediction came true.'"

Bach, who wore No. 17, played only one year for the Celtics, coming off the bench to average 3.5 points a game. He was cut during training camp the following season when rookie Joe Mullaney, who would eventually enjoy a highly successful pro and college coaching career, beat him out for the final roster spot.

"Because of my love for the game, I decided to play for Hartford in the eastern Basketball League. We got $100 a game, and we usually played three or four times a week," Bach remembers. "The competition was excellent. The New York Rens, an all-black team, had about five players who could have been All-Star types in the NBA had it not been for the league's racial discrimination policy. In fact, the Rens had a 6'3" shooter named Pops Gates who was as good an all-around player as anybody in the NBA. Today, he's in the Hall of Fame because everyone knew how talented he was.

"The Rens faced racial bias in every city they played, yet they maintained the highest degree of professionalism. Today, I have a picture of the Rens squad hanging in my office, and I tell all the black players that they owe a debt to those guys because they paved the way for blacks to play in the NBA. One of the Rens players, Chuck Cooper, was among the first blacks drafted by the league, chosen by Walter Brown and the great Red Auerbach."

Shortly after the 1949-'50 Eastern League season had ended, Bach was offered the opportunity to become the head coach at Fordham, his alma mater. "I really didn't think I was qualified for the job because I had no experience," he says, "but the athletic director convinced me to give it a try." In Bach's first five years on the Fordham bench, the Rams compiled a record of 95-39, never losing more than nine games in any one season.

"Everything about the situation was great," he says. "I had some great teams there. In '67, though, I had to leave because I wasn't making enough money to support my wife, Mary, and our five children. I accepted an offer to coach Penn State, where I received a better salary. I was also given tenure for teaching, which paid extra."

The strangest day in Bach's coaching career came in 1972. "I was an assistant to Henry Iba on the U.S. Olympic team," he says. "That was, of course, the team which supposedly lost to the Soviet Union in the final three seconds of the Gold Medal game because of three controversial ruling by the officials. I have never seen such a complete injustice."

After guiding the Nittany Lions to a 122-121 record over a 10-year span, Bach asked for a leave of absence. "I knew I would probably never go back to college coaching. All the recruiting had burnt me out," he explained. "I realized I would never want to deal with recruiting again. I had my pilot's license, so I went to work flying planes for the Piper Corporation."

When then-Golden State Warriors General Manager Pete Newell asked Bach to become head coach Al Attles's top assistant, Bach jumped at the chance to get back into the sport he loved.

"Pete and Al were both people I knew and respected," he says. "I had only been away from the game for a year, but I really missed coaching. Now I'd be back—on the pro level, something I hadn't done yet. It was the challenge I was looking for."

Shortly before the start of the 1983-'84 season, Attles moved into the front office, and Bach was promoted to head coach. "We had three tough years because we weren't very deep," he says of the experience. "Larry Smith was a monster as a power forward. Purvis Short, with that rainbow shot of his, and Sleepy Floyd gave us outside scoring. Beyond that, we lacked consistency, especially at center where Joe Barry Carroll had been a disappointment.

When Bach was dismissed by the Warriors in the summer of '86, he faced a major dilemma. "I could play the waiting game and sit at home until someone offered me a head coach's job, or I could find an assistant's position. I knew that if I waited for a head coaching opening, it would probably be with a team which was having big-time problems. That's how it always works out in the pros. In military terms, it boiled down to this: Did I want to be the leader of a barbarian outfit or did I want to be a captain in the Roman Army?"

Bach chose the latter, joining Phil Jackson (and Michael Jordan, of course) in Chicago. When the Bulls reeled off three straight titles in 1991, '92, and '93, it was Bach who designed and directed the defense.

"Those were great, great times," he says. "You know, I had always thought Oscar Robertson was the one NBA player who stood above everyone who ever played the game. Michael, however, was better than Oscar. He was absolutely peerless."

Leaving Chicago in 1994, Bach spent two seasons in Charlotte, two in Detroit, and three in Washington as an assistant. "I was all set to retire," he says, "but then one of my former players, [Bulls General Manager] Johnny Paxson, called me and asked me to join [new head coach] Scott Skiles's staff. I couldn't say no to Johnny."

Bach, who lives in the outskirts of Chicago with his wife, Mary, a practicing lawyer, calls his career more fun than an amusement park. "It's been one adventure after another, right from my first days in Boston," he says. "Things couldn't have gone much better than I had it."

His favorite souvenir from all his years in coaching is not one of the championship rings he earned in the NBA, but rather a letter he once received from Bob Cousy when the Celtic Hall of Famer was coaching Boston College.

"I was coaching Fordham and we had just beaten BC at their place. It was a big win for us because they had a darn good squad," Bach says. "A few days later, a letter arrived at my office. It said, 'Last time I saw you, you were being lifted to the heavens by your players and fans. Congratulations on a job well done. Best wishes, Bob.' I was amazed that someone as busy as Cousy would take the time to write such a nice message. I still have that letter, which is my most treasured basketball possession."

So, Bach was prepared to become a couch potato—until a friend of his asked him to coach a wheelchair basketball team for a season. "I was astounded at the players' skills, but it was a different type of game, one I never could adjust to even though I admired the team's hustle and enthusiasm," he says. "The players needed a coach who understood the finer points of wheelchair basketball better than I did.

"Just when I thought I was finally officially retired, John Quinn, the brother of Pat Quinn, the governor of Illinois, asked me to become a volunteer assistant for the Fenwick High boys team. I couldn't refuse. I've been there four years now and I love every minute. The kids want to learn. They respect the coaches. They respect the game," he says. "They're easier to teach than the pros. As long as I have my health, I'm planning on being on the bench. I'm not setting any goals, but I'm 87 and now 90 sounds like a nice round number."

Where Have You Gone?

ERNIE BARRETT

The Gift

ERNIE BARRETT

**College: Kansas State | Height: 6'3" | Weight: 180 lbs.
DOB: 12/27/1929 | Years with Celtics: 1953-'54 and 1955-'56
Position: Guard**

Notes: Nicknamed "Black Jack." Played collegiate basketball at Kansas State. Barrett earned All-America honors for the 1951 team that posted a 25-4 record and advanced all the way to the NCAA championship game under coach Jack Gardner. First round draft choice of the Boston Celtics in 1951. Played two seasons for the Celtics. Later became the Athletic Director at Kansas State. Number 22 jersey was retired by Kansas State in 2005. Ernie Barrett Athletic Endowment Society named in his honor.

His basketball career began in a Kansas railroad town, and while his legacy will forever be defined by his contributions to Kansas State University—first as an All-American guard with a feathery touch from outside, and then as the school's athletic director and fund-raiser extraordinaire—Ernie Barrett will also remain deeply woven into the fabric of professional basketball's greatest franchise. Selected in the first round of the 1951 NBA Draft by Red Auerbach and the Boston Celtics, Barrett's most important contribution may have come years later, as Auerbach

53

wrestled over whom to select with the Number 4 overall pick in 1970—
New Mexico State big man Sam Lacey, or Florida State's undersized-but-
energetic Dave Cowens. Auerbach respected Barrett's opinion immensely.
He also knew that Barrett, then the K-State athletic director, had seen
Lacey in action against the Wildcats. Barrett came away from that contest
less than enamored with the Aggies' 6'10" center, and he shared his
evaluation with Auerbach on the eve of the draft. The Celtics patriarch
heeded Barrett's advice and selected Cowens at Number 4. While Lacey
would go on to play thirteen solid-yet-unspectacular seasons with the
Cincinnati Royals, New York Knicks, New Jersey Nets, and Cleveland
Cavaliers, Cowens would win two NBA championships with Boston and
wind up in the Naismith Memorial Basketball Hall of Fame.

Today, the energetic 82-year-old Barrett is the retired Director of
Development for Kansas State Athletics. Under his watch, Barrett was
instrumental in raising money for major improvements to the K-State
sports facilities, such as new additions to the Vanier Sports Complex, as well
as to the improvement of facilities for the football, volleyball, basketball,
and track teams. He credits his education in public relations for helping
him become a better communicator in his current position.

"The ability to communicate effectively is important in fund raising,"
he says emphatically. "It helps open doors and checkbooks, both of which
are very important when soliciting donations for projects that cost millions."

Although he officially stepped away from this post in 2010, Barrett is
still closely connected to fund raising at K-State. He remains involved via
the Ernie Barrett Athletic Endowment Society, a segment of the school's
fund raising efforts that bears his name. The Society is a fully implemented
athletic endowment program at Kansas State University, and represents a
long-term solution to the ever-escalating costs of competing in the ultra-
competitive world of intercollegiate athletics.

Barrett is especially proud of a project that is currently underway,
the construction of a new, 50,000 square foot Basketball Training Facility,
which will include two practice courts, locker rooms (men's and women's),
players lounges, coaches offices, a 2,500 square foot weight room, a sports
medicine center, and a team film room.

"Kansas State has been blessed with a great basketball coliseum, but it was built as a multi-purpose facility and has been limited in terms of practice development. Now we have the opportunity to add a training facility that will keep the great basketball tradition alive at Kansas State!"

Barrett may have grown up in the shadow of the Great Depression, but the hard times did little to dampen his can-do spirit or quell his outsized personality, gifts that have served him well throughout an illustrious career capped by a statue in his honor and the unofficial title of "Mr. K-State." His palm-crushing handshake has become both his calling card and the stuff of legend. Years earlier that calling card was his dead-eye shooting, a gift that helped propel a tiny Kansas high school to its only state basketball championship and earn Barrett a scholarship to Kansas State University.

"We won the state championship in 1947," Barrett says, "which is still the last time a team from Wellington has won a state title in basketball. That '47 Wellington squad had plenty of talent, fine players like Harold Rogers who went on to play for coach [Henry] Iba at Oklahoma State University. Our coach was John Floyd, and I credit him with all of my success as a basketball player. He was the person who taught me the fundamentals, and the one who really helped me to improve my shooting. I was a 6'1" center in high school—that should tell you about the height we had on that team—and I went on to play guard at Kansas State. I probably wouldn't have made it as a college player if Coach Floyd hadn't worked with me on my outside shooting. Even back then you just didn't find many 6'1" centers playing major college basketball [laughs]. K-State had a 6'5" guard that first year I was on the team, and the Boston Celtics had players like Bob Donham who were bigger than me. So learning to play away from the basket was a tremendous help, and Coach Floyd was the person who had the most to do with that development."

Barrett joined the Wildcats in 1947, the same season legendary coach Jack Gardner—who would later earn the distinction as the only coach to take two schools to the Final Four twice—returned to the helm at K-State. The union proved just the tonic for the once-moribund basketball program, as the Wildcats improved their win total by 10 games and posted a winning season for the first time in sixteen years. By 1951 the circle was complete; K-State toppled mighty Oklahoma State before battling Adolph Rupp's Kentucky Wildcats in the Final Four title game. UK may have won that game, shutting down K-State with rock-hard defense in the second half, but Barrett capped his dream season in style; the talented senior received All-American honors, and quickly found himself the draft-day property of the Boston Celtics.

"Unfortunately I injured my shoulder against Oklahoma State in the West Regional Final in Kansas City—there were only two regionals then—and wasn't able to play to my fullest against Kentucky. We beat BYU 64-54 in the semifinals and then defeated Oklahoma State to advance to the championship game. It was the worst defeat Coach Iba had ever suffered at Oklahoma State. I took a charge in that game and ended up with a deep muscle bruise. We were going to shoot it up with Novocain but Coach Gardner was against it—he thought it might be injurious to my health, and he didn't want to cause any long-term damage to the shoulder.

"Kentucky was coached by Rupp, and they had some really great players on that team. They had Bill Spivey, who scored 22 points in that game, and a couple of other pretty good players in Cliff Hagan and Frank Ramsey. We jumped out to an early lead and were up by two at the half, 29-27, but couldn't hold them off after intermission. Kentucky dominated the boards and won the game by 10 (68-58)."

Barrett joined a Celtics team boasting a fiery, young coach named Red Auerbach, but the arrival of the great Bill Russell was still several years away. The league was still in its infancy. Fans flocked to the college game, while the NBA struggled to attract a mainstream audience and earn a place alongside baseball and football as one of the country's major professional sports. Players such as Barrett were vital in this regard; they possessed valuable name recognition, a key component in selling the league to a reluctant public. Barrett, however, did not immediately join the Celtics.

"I had a two-year military obligation," he explains, "so my 'rookie' year was actually two years later [1953-'54]. Red started me every game during the exhibition season, opposite Bob Cousy, for what amounted to 15-20 games over a three week period. We basically barnstormed all over New England.

"Things changed once the regular season started. I didn't get into a single game during the first 35 games, at which point [Celtic owner] Walter Brown went to Red and wanted to know why I wasn't playing. He [Brown] looked at me as the team's first round selection in 1951 and figured I should be seeing some action. Needless to say, I was on Walter Brown's side. So I ended up playing more during the second half of the season, sharing time with the great Bill Sharman."

Despite the lack of playing time, Barrett and Auerbach developed a strong relationship that lasts to this day.

"Coach Auerbach amazed me with the way he handled the players," says Barrett, "and with how he was able to keep them all happy and ready to play. He knew which players responded well to the screaming, and he knew which ones to motivate in a more subtle way. There really is no comparison between Red and anyone else. He was extremely intelligent, a real genius."

As for the late Auerbach, he clearly respected and valued Barrett's opinion. Drafting Cowens is a prime example.

"That's exactly how it happened," Barrett replies, when asked about the dynamics behind Boston's Number 4 selection in the 1970 NBA Draft. "I saw Sam Lacey, so I knew what he was capable of—not to say that he couldn't play, but I just thought Cowens had much better mobility and could shoot the ball better. Red was leaning toward choosing Lacey, and he called to ask who I thought was the better player. To me, Cowens was a perfect fit in the Celtics' system. He could get up and down the court, and he could run all day long. And he was intense. Red took my advice, and it worked out well for everyone involved."

Unlikely to take a starting job from either Cousy or Sharman, Barrett returned to Kansas following the season determined to begin a career in coaching. The stay would be short-lived, as the NBA adopted the 24-second shot clock following the 1954-'55 season. Auerbach, sensing that the change would be a boon to free-wheeling, dead-eye players like Barrett, wasted little time in placing a call to coax the All-American out of retirement. Barrett gladly accepted, playing one more successful season in a Celtics uniform before returning to his beloved

K-State for good. (The 1955-'56 Boston Celtics averaged a league-high 106 points-per-game, with super-sub Barrett averaging 20.2 minutes-per-game off the bench.)

"I wanted to play—I'm a competitor," says Barrett. "Red thought that this change suited my style of play, so he asked me to come back. I said that I would, but only if I got a chance to play. Red was true to his word—I played in every game that season. I really wanted to stay on, but the next season the Celtics got Heinsohn and Russell. Tex Winter was the head coach at K-State at the time, and he offered me a position as assistant coach. I jumped at the opportunity, and I went to work at my alma mater. I've been there ever since."

Barrett's name is indelibly linked to Kansas State University, his legend there secure. He has been inducted into the K-State Athletic Hall of Fame, both as a player and as an administrator. He has been part and parcel of the university for six decades, first as an All-America basketball player, later as the athletics director and now as fund-raiser extraordinaire. His jersey was retired by the school in 2005. Still, he remains closely connected to the Boston Celtics. He counts Bob Cousy among his closest friends, and his relationship with the late Auerbach is especially noteworthy. Barrett played alongside Celtic tough man Bob Brannum in his first stint with the team, and then played with "Jungle" Jim Loscutoff two years later. And then there is Dave Cowens. Had Auerbach selected Lacey, those championships in 1974 and 1976—banners twelve and thirteen on your scorecard—probably wouldn't have happened at all. Barrett's advice validated Auerbach's faith in his one-time sharpshooter, and proved to be the perfect gift indeed.

Where Have You Gone?

NATE ARCHIBALD

Nothing "Tiny" about His Achievements

NATE ARCHIBALD

College: Texas-El Paso | Height: 6'1" | Weight: 165 lbs.
DOB: 09/02/1948
Position: Guard
Years with Celtics: 1978-1983

Notes: A playground legend while growing up in the South Bronx. Chosen in the second round of the 1970 NBA draft. Also drafted by the Dallas Chapparals of the American Basketball Association. Only NBA player to lead the league in scoring and assists in the same season (1972-'73).

When Nate "Tiny" Archibald was traded to Boston by the San Diego Clippers in the summer of 1978, he wasn't certain he'd make it through even one year in a Celtics uniform. Having missed the entire previous season while recovering from a torn Achilles tendon, the former three-time All-Star justifiably wondered whether, at age 30, he was ancient history. The Celtics, attempting to mount a comeback of their own after going 30-52, were willing to gamble that Archibald's fierce competitive nature would eventually drive him to become the "Tiny" of old.

"Fortunately for me, Red [Auerbach] was completely in my corner right from the start," the now 64-year-old Hall of Famer explains. "Before training camp, he just looked me right in the eyes and said, 'Look, there's no sense in pushing yourself too much and risking a setback. I want you back at 100 percent, not 70 or 80 percent. Don't worry about this season, because we're going to stink, with or without you.' And, boy, was he right. Things were pretty ugly during my first year [in Boston]."

Indisputably, Archibald had once been the NBA's premiere point guard, a clever, intelligent, and mentally tough floor leader. His game was both explosive and fundamentally sound, two descriptions that in today's basketball world be a contradiction in terms. Proof positive of his overall offensive talents came in 1973 when the 6'1" Archibald set a "virtually untouchable" record by leading the league in both scoring (34.0 points a game) and assists (11.4 per game) in the same season as a member of the

Kansas City Kings, not coincidentally coached by another playmaking genius, Bob Cousy, who had selected the University of Texas at El Paso star in second round of the 1970 draft.

"I don't see Tiny's record being broken," says Cousy. "Today's teams don't get enough easy fastbreak baskets. They'd rather run a set offense and have their big star go one-on-one. Unless coaches go back to a faster paced, more wide-open game, Tiny's record is as safe as any. And what makes that record so impressive to me is that Tiny had a pass-first mentality. He certainly wasn't a gunner. The vast majority of his points came off drives to the basket where he'd either get a layup or give up that frail body of his to draw a foul. When he did take a jumper from the outside, it was an open shot. He'd take them and make most of them just to keep his defender off-balance."

The pupil has equally high praise for his first pro coach. "Cousy had faith in me, a lot more than I had in myself as a 21-year-old," recalls Archibald. "He just handed me the ball and said, 'This is your team. Run the show.' A lot of guys get drafted a lot higher than I was and don't play at all their first year. Here I was as a no-name rookie, thinking how lucky I was just to be in the league, starting as the point guard. I did what Cooz asked, but I wasn't ready for it. I made more than my share of mistakes, but Cooz would never be anything but positive. It was his coaching which set up my whole career."

But in 1978, as a new member of the Celtics, the lefty guard—all 160 pounds of him—would have to prove to the experts and, more importantly, to himself that he could fit in, still lead a team, and stay healthy. "I had a lot of self-doubt about my speed and quickness," Archibald recalls. "In the back of your mind, you always have thoughts about blowing out the tendon again. The only thing I didn't worry about were the fundamentals. I knew I still had my skills to carry me."

Playing in 69 games, Archibald averaged just 11.0 points and 4.7 assists, both career lows, in his first Celtic season. "I can't say I was satisfied with how I played, but I could live with it. We were one of the worst rebounding teams in the league, so we didn't have much of a fastbreak game," he says with a wry smile. "Our whole offensive game was weak.

There was too much individual play and not enough passing. We won just 29 games. . . . Red was right. We did sort of stink."

Still, Archibald was optimistic about his future. "By the end of the season, I was completely healthy. I knew my Achilles problem was in the past," he explains. "For the first time in more than two years, I had no injury issues. I could finally concentrate on just playing. After our final game, Red sat down with me and told me what he wanted me to work on in the offseason. I knew he wanted me back, but he didn't make any promises."

On the day it was announced that former Cavs coach Bill Fitch would take over on the Celtics bench, Archibald received a phone call. "Fitch told me I would be starting," says Archibald, who, as a four-year-old, was nicknamed "Tiny" by his father. "Then he told me to be in 'running shape' because he wanted a fastbreak team. Right then, given how we had walked the ball up the court in '78-'79, I knew there were going to be a lot of new faces around."

Including one Larry Joe Bird.

"Because [Bird] was drafted a year before he signed, I had seen him play in college a number of times. I remember there were people who said he can't run, can't jump, and has no quickness," says Archibald. "My reaction was 'Who cares?' The guy did everything right fundamentally. He shot perfectly, passed perfectly, rebounded perfectly. When he showed how good he was as a pro, people started calling him 'Larry Legend.' I always said he was 'Larry The Professor,' because if you watched him, you could learn everything there is to know about how to play the game."

Along with Bird, the Celtics also added second-year center Rick Robey, veteran swingman M. L. Carr, and rookie guard Gerald Henderson. "Even in training camp, which was definitely hell, I knew we had a serious team. It all stemmed from how Bird played the game," Archibald says. "I mean, he'd do something in every game, even in practice, that would make me shake my head and wonder, 'Damn, how did he do that?' When you have a guy who plays with as much confidence as Bird did, everybody just picks up on it."

With Bird earning Rookie of the Year honors, Boston was able to achieve the greatest one-season turnaround in NBA history, going from an embarrassing 29 wins in 1979 to 61 victories in 1980. It was a rebirth not only for the Celtics, but for their point guard, too, who was named to the All-Star team for the first time since 1976. Playing 37 minutes a game and averaging 14.1 points and 8.4 assists, Archibald wore down the opposition with his brilliance as the floor leader.

"We had a bunch of guys who loved to rebound and take off running," remembers Archibald. "Max [Cedric Maxwell], [Dave] Cowens, Bird, and Robey, they all could go to the boards, make the outlet pass, and beat their man upcourt. That made my job easy because, as the point person, I had a lot of options."

In the Eastern Conference Finals, however, the Celtics were humbled by the Julius Erving-led 76ers, who utilized a well-balanced halfcourt offense to limit Boston's running opportunities and take the series, 4-1. "To get that far and then go totally flat, it was embarrassing," says Archibald. "That whole offseason people asked me the same question I was asking myself: 'What happened?' I didn't have any good answers."

With Boston acquiring Robert Parish and the draft rights to power forward Kevin McHale in The Great Golden State Swindle, Archibald now had two additional offensive weapons at his disposal as the Celtics opened up the 1980-'81 season. "This team had no weaknesses. And because of how we finished up the previous year, we were hungry, even a bit cocky," Archibald explains. "As Maxwell used to tell us when the game was on the line, 'If you're scared, better buy yourself a Doberman.' Well, we weren't scared of anybody."

The Celtics and rival Philly both won 62 games in the regular season. Then the two teams again faced each other in the conference finals. Down 3-1, the Celtics staged what is considered the NBA's most exciting and greatest comeback, winning the final three games of the series by a total of five points.

"I still remember Red coming into the locker room in Philadelphia after we had lost Game 4. We were all upset, but he was very calm," recalls Archibald. "He looked at us for a second and then told us, 'Look, this series isn't over. They still have to win one more game to beat you. One more game. Don't let them win that one more game. It's that simple.' And that's how we approached the rest of the series."

The championship matchup against the Houston Rockets was truly anticlimactic, with the Celtics winning championship No. 14 in six games as Tiny's penetration moves produced 13 points and 12 assists in the clincher.

"Without a doubt, the greatest moment in my career," says Archibald. "To be a part of that team with all the great players we had is something I am very proud of. The year I led the league in points and assists doesn't compare to being on a championship team, because I didn't help the Kings win a thing. We didn't even make the playoffs the year I set that record. That's why individual stats have never impressed me too much."

Compiling a 63-19 regular-season record the following year, the Celtics seemed to be on track for a title repeat. However, in Game 3 of the Conference Finals against the 76ers, Archibald suffered what would be a series-ending left shoulder injury. Without its backcourt leader, Boston fell to Philly in seven games.

"Very depressing," Archibald recalls. "I couldn't raise my shooting arm. I even practiced shooting righty, but I knew I couldn't help the team."

Archibald's Celtic career came to an abrupt and contentious end following Milwaukee's four-game sweep of Boston in the 1983 Eastern Conference semifinals. Fitch had decided to use the 34-year-old playmaker as the sixth man rather than a starter in the Bucks series. Although the coach stressed that the move would enable Archibald to be fresher and more productive in crucial moments of the game, especially during crunch time, the veteran guard was quietly fuming. "I wouldn't mind if someone beat me out for my starter's role. But to just have it taken away . . . that's not right," he said moments before the disastrous series began.

Two months after the Celtics' collapse against the Bucks, the six-time All-Star was unceremoniously waived. He finished his career by playing 51 games with Milwaukee the following season before quietly retiring. "It wasn't the way I hoped to go out," he says, "but I had a great career doing what I loved."

Not surprisingly, a primary focus of Archibald's life after pro basketball is helping inner-city youths understand the importance of gaining an education. As a player, Archibald would spend his off-seasons coaching youth basketball in the South Bronx, where he had grown up.

"It's not a pretty neighborhood. Many of the buildings are completely burnt out. There's poverty, crime, and drugs everywhere," he says. "It's hard for kids here to realize that the world can open up to them. That's one of the things I emphasize, that they can improve themselves through basketball, but more importantly, by getting an education."

Said South Bronx community worker Hilton Barker, "Once [basketball players] make it, they're gone. Once they get the big car, they point it out of here. Except for Tiny. He came back."

But not merely to teach basketball. Even today, it is not unusual for Archibald to spend his summer nights buying pizza and soda for kids and just talking to them for hours about subjects ranging from music to school to drug use.

"Because I was a pro athlete, kids listen to me," he explains. "My big advantage is that I'm in the community every chance I get. No one drools over me. Because of what I've done with my life, they listen to me. When they need help, they know they can come to me without being shy, because I'm just a guy who hangs around with them. We're on the same level. It's just friend-to-friend relationships.

"I don't preach to the kids, I just talk with them. I tell them about opportunities for scholarships, student loans, and grants—even if they don't play basketball. I'm realistic, though. I know I can't help everybody. You might have a group of 15 kids, and only two or three will make it to some degree of success. It's just a sad fact that some of them are not going to be able to leave [the South Bronx]."

Given his dedication to helping youngsters both on and off the basketball court, it is not surprising that Archibald, after spending five years as an assistant coach at Georgia, decided to pursue a career in education. After obtaining his master's degree from Fordham University in 1990 and his Professional Diploma in Supervision and Administration in 1994, Archibald became a teacher at P.S. 175 in the Bronx. In his spare time, he worked at the Harlem Men's Shelter.

A member of the NBA's 50th Anniversary All-Time Team and a Hall of Famer, Archibald has coached in the ABA, NBDL, and, most recently, the USBL with the Brevard Blue Ducks. But no one has given him the opportunity to coach at the NBA level. "I'd certainly listen to any offers," he says, "but there just haven't been any yet, and I'm not getting any younger."

The problem, according to Cousy, is that NBA coaches still belong to a "Good Old Boys" fraternity. "Tiny's quiet. He isn't a self-promoter or a guy who 'networks.' He's not the type of person who walks into a room with a big smile and starts shaking hands with everybody. He's still shy, maybe somewhat insecure. His personality may hurt him in his quest to be a NBA coach. What's obvious is that he has a great knowledge of the game and he can communicate that knowledge, especially to younger players. He'd make a hell of a coach if someone would give him the chance."

While he waits for an opportunity, which he knows is a longshot, Archibald works part-time in the NBA's community relations department. He continues to coach youth basketball in both Harlem and the South Bronx.

"I'm not a big fan of AAU programs," he says. "Coaches go all out to recruit the best talent. Then they just go and throw a ball onto the court and say, 'Okay, start playing.' Their teams win, but the kids themselves lose because they aren't learning a thing about the fundamentals of the game. That's not what youth basketball should be about."

A college coach, he says, shouldn't judge his successes and failures by wins and losses but by how many of his players graduate, by how many of his players come out of college prepared for the rest of their lives. "Everybody wants to talk about Kevin Garnett, Kobe Bryant, and LeBron James, kids who went to the NBA directly from high school. Now kids who want to play in the NBA have to play a year in college or go overseas before they're eligible for the draft. What's ignored by the league, the fans, and the agents are the hundreds of kids who leave after their freshman or sophomore years and then wash out after a year or two in the NBA, the NBDL, or overseas. When these kids can't make it big, they have no clue what to do with the rest of their lives," Archibald says. "In the NFL, at least kids stay in college for three or four years before turning pro. They get the chance to get at least a good start on a college education."

Currently residing in the New York City area, Archibald continues to lead by example. Now 64 years old, he has been accepted for the doctorate program at Fordham. "Getting my PhD would be my greatest accomplishment in life. I'm no Einstein, and I'm not smarter than anyone else, but maybe I've been more persistent. I'd like to be known as a teacher and a mentor more than a former All-Star pro basketball player. I want to show kids that if they are determined to reach their goal, whatever it might be, anything is achievable."

Where Have You Gone?

RON BONHAM

A Wild Life

RON BONHAM

College: Cincinnati | Height: 6'5" | Weight: 200 lbs.
DOB: 05/31/1942 | Years with Celtics: 1964-'65 through 1965-'66
Position: Guard

Notes: Twice a first-team All-State player at Muncie Central High School (Indiana). Indiana's Mr. Basketball in 1960. Helped University of Cincinnati to one national championship, and to the runner-up spot the next season. First team All-American as a junior, second team as a senior. Second round draft choice by the Boston Celtics (the 16th pick overall) in 1964. Member of two NBA World Championship teams with the Celtics (1965 and 1966). Member of the first Indiana Pacers team (ABA).

It has been more than forty years since he traded basketball hardwood for the hardwood in and around his native Muncie, Indiana, his love affair with the outdoors carrying him worlds away from all those musty old NBA stadiums and annual championship celebrations with the Boston Celtics. Not that he's missed it. As funny as that might sound to those who have dreamed of donning a jersey and playing for their favorite NBA team, Ron Bonham actually couldn't wait to walk away from basketball fame and reconnect with Mother Nature. Following his retirement from professional

69

hoops as an original member of the ABA's Indiana Pacers, the one-time Mr. Basketball spent 38 years as the superintendent at Prairie Creek Park, 2,300 acres of fun and recreation for those looking to get away from it all.

"My dad was an outdoors person," says Ron Bonham, still a basketball legend in his basketball-crazed Hoosier state. "He more or less raised me on the river. We fished and hunted all the time. He taught me how to appreciate nature, and how to respect the environment. Being in the outdoors is something I've always been passionate about, so getting back to nature was the perfect fit for me. It has made for a great life."

And now, more than three years after his 2008 retirement from the parks system, Bonham is as appreciative and respectful than ever. He knows that he is the exception, that rare person who was able to spend his entire life doing what he loved most, first as a decorated athlete and then as the chief caretaker at his beloved Prairie Creek Reservoir and Campground.

"I've been lucky. The opportunity to work at Prairie Creek Reservoir came along at the perfect time for me, as I was getting out of basketball, and I thoroughly enjoyed my time working there. I had a good, long run, serving as the superintendent for 38 years before stepping away in November, 2008. My wife worked at the same facility for more than 35 years. So it has been good. I had plenty of other opportunities to make double or triple the money that I made working there, but, like that old catchphrase, there are some things that money can't buy."

While fortune may not have been in the cards, fame has followed Bonham since his playing days at Muncie Central High School. Known affectionately as the 'Blonde Bomber' and the 'Muncie Mortar,' Bonham finished his career as the leading scorer in the history of Indiana high school basketball with 2,023 points. As a senior he averaged 28 points-per-game. Bonham was twice a first-team All-State player, and in 1960 he was named Mr. Basketball in the State of Indiana.

"That was a great honor," Bonham says. "I was also lucky enough to be named MVP of both the Indiana and Kentucky All-Star games."

Bonham is quick to point out that team goals have always been more important than individual accomplishments.

"We had a lot of talent on our high school team. We were the top-ranked team in the state during my senior year, and we won 29 straight games to reach the state championship. We lost that game. That defeat will always be the biggest disappointment of my life as a basketball player, because we had some phenomenal talent on that team. All five starters would go on to play Division I college basketball—our starting point guard was the state champion in the low hurdles—so that shows you what kind of talent we had."

Bonham had his pick of colleges following his stellar career at Muncie Central. With over 300 scholarship offers on the table, he ultimately decided to follow the path of another Indiana high school legend—Oscar Robertson—to the University of Cincinnati.

"It was a hard decision," says Bonham. "I talked it over with my parents, and we narrowed it down to two schools—Cincinnati and Purdue. Attending a basketball school was important to me. Purdue was known more as a football power, and the University of Cincinnati was a power basketball program. And with Oscar being there—he was a senior in college when I was a senior in high school—I just couldn't pass up the opportunity to play for the Bearcats."

As a freshman, Bonham would watch UC win the national championship. (At the time, freshmen were not permitted to play varsity sports.) The Bearcats would repeat a year later with Bonham on the court. Denied a championship in high school, he was suddenly on top of the basketball world.

"What a thrill to win it all," says Bonham. "You just can't put it into words. During my freshman season we ran a run-and-shoot offense, but then the coaching situation changed due to health issues. We played at a slower pace, buckled down on defense, and adopted a completely different philosophy toward the game. This was all new to me, because we had played the run-and-shoot in high school. But I can't complain. The end result was well worth it."

The Bearcats were back in the title game after Bonham's junior season, where they were upset by Loyola of Chicago.

"We were ranked Number 1 in the nation," says Bonham, "and we were winning the game handily. We went into our stall with about 10 minutes in the game, which we usually didn't do until there were five or six minutes left, and the momentum changed. We threw the ball away, made too many mistakes, and just didn't handle their zone press very well. Loyola came back and forced overtime. We should have had three national championships in a row, but we let it get away from us."

A two-time All-America selection at Cincinnati, Bonham then found himself drafted by Red Auerbach and the Boston Celtics. He had never been so far away from home.

"I don't know how much my phone bill was," he says, laughing. "But I called home several times a week and would talk for hours."

A great athlete, Bonham was nevertheless ill-prepared for those grueling training camps ran by Auerbach.

"I was talking to Red on the phone after the draft, and he says, 'Bonham, you're going to be in the best shape of your life.' At the time, I thought I was already in great shape. In high school I worked out six hours a day. In college I kept myself in peak condition. But then I went to Boston, where there were three openings and between 50 and 60 people competing for those spots. After that first day with Auerbach, there were just a handful of people who came back. I can remember Tommy Heinsohn being carried off the floor after that practice because he'd passed out. But that was Auerbach's way. He wanted to see if you really wanted it."

Bonham survived Auerbach's boot camp, making the cut along with fellow rookie Mel Counts. The Celtics roared out of the blocks; the 62 wins that season were a club record, and the club won its seventh consecutive NBA championship. That 1964-'65 season was not without adversity, however, as team founder Walter Brown passed away on September 7, 1964.

"That was my first year coming in, so I didn't get to know Walter that well," he says. "But everything about that franchise was first class—the travel, the hotel accommodations, everything. It spoiled me, because I was on that first Indiana Pacer team when it was in the ABA. It was the exact opposite. We sat in airports all night long, things like that. Just a lot of disorganization. That was never the case with the Celtics, and all of the credit goes to Walter Brown."

And while Brown may have owned the team and ensured quality travel arrangements, it was Auerbach who handled the contract negotiations with the players.

"Mel Counts and I went in to sign our first contracts," he recalls, laughing, "and we walk into Red's office. Here he was with his feet up on his desk, smoking his cigar, and the smoke was as thick as a cloud. Well, he takes his feet off the desk, grabs two pieces of paper and shoves them at Mel and I. Then he says, 'This ain't a democracy. Here is what you boys are going to get this year.'"

As a rookie, little did Bonham know that he would witness basketball history firsthand. He was watching from the bench as John Havlicek stole the ball from the Philadelphia 76ers in the 1965 Eastern Conference Finals.

"That whole series was a knockdown, drag-out battle," says Bonham. "I can remember Bill Russell trying to throw the ball in and hitting the guide wire in the process. We were all going crazy on the sidelines. And for Johnny Havlicek to make that play, that was one of the greatest moments I've ever been part of as a basketball player. And of course you had the famous call by Johnny Most. It doesn't get much better than that."

The Celtics dismantled the Lakers 4-1 to secure the team's seventh consecutive title—and eighth overall. While this may have been old hat to players like Bill Russell and Sam Jones, it was a new experience for Bonham.

"Oh boy, what a great thrill. It was such an honor to be a part of something like that. I remember leaving the court after that last game, and the crowd was going wild. Johnny Havlicek and I somehow got off the beaten trail on the way to the locker room, and our warm-up jackets get ripped off our bodies by the fans. Then our jerseys get ripped off. Then I felt someone grab hold of my trunks, and I thought those were going to get ripped off [laughs]. Finally some security people got around us and led us back to the dressing room. If it weren't for them, we may have lost all of our clothes before we made it back there [laughs]."

Red Auerbach would bow out the following season with yet another championship, the team's eighth in a row. The starting five had an average age of 31 that season, and many experts felt the team was too old to win again. How were the Celtics able to overcome the age factor to win yet again?

"We were family," he says, "and a very talented one at that. I remember my first year with the team, and Bill Russell didn't speak to any of the rookies or the news guys coming in to compete for a spot on the team. Havlicek and I had been friends all through college, and I asked John about Bill. John said that that's just the way he is. He said that if you make the team, then Bill treats you like one of the family—and that's exactly the way it happened for me. After I made the team it was just like night and day. Russell and his wife would invite us over to their house for dinner, or over to his soul food restaurant in downtown Boston, and he made you feel like a part of the family. So the talent was there, and the love for one another was there. That really made the age factor irrelevant."

After two world championships with the Celtics, Bonham signed with the Pacers of the fledgling ABA. He retired from professional basketball in 1968, and was at Prairie Creek Reservoir less than a year later. Along the way he served three four-year terms as county commissioner, built a new home on a 60-acre tract of land just east of the reservoir, and opened a kennel for Springer Spaniels.

And in 1991, he was inducted into the Indiana Basketball Hall of Fame.

"What a great honor," he says, smiling. "Indiana is the cradle of basketball. It's a religion in this state. To be inducted into the hall of fame is very special to me."

And does he miss overseeing Prairie Creek Park?

"It's in good hands. I still keep tabs on it, though. It's hard not to, when you've been attached for something for so long."

What would be the biggest challenge facing this pristine park going forward?

"Over the years I've seen more and more construction, more traffic. It's just natural. People are drawn to the water. The want to build close enough to the water to be able to see it. As a result, there have been a lot of big houses going up in the surrounding area. The City of Muncie's lease on the property expires in 2021, so the big thing is to protect it after the lease expires. People that I talk to don't want multi-million-dollar homes built on the waterfront. They want nature trails and wildlife habitat."

What does the future hold for this former Boston Celtic?

"Enjoy life, enjoy the outdoors," he says. "Our home is situated in a state wildlife habitat. We have an abundance of quail, and several years ago we put in a six acre wetland. We still travel to North Dakota a couple of times a year to hunt, and vacation in Iowa several times a year as well. I'm enjoying life. The timing was right for me to ride off into the sunset."

For a man who loves wildlife, it has been a very rich life indeed.

GENE CONLEY

Two-Sport Champion

GENE CONLEY

College: Washington State | Height: 6'9" | Weight: 230 lbs.
DOB: 11/10/1930 | Position: Center/Power Forward
Years with Celtics: 1952-'53, 1958-'59 through 1960-'61

Notes: Member of three Boston Celtics championship team. Also was three-time National League All-Star. Was winning pitcher in 1955 All-Star Game. Member of the World Series champion Milwaukee Braves in 1957.

When Gene Conley tried out for the Boston Celtics in 1952, it was a decision largely motivated by the fact that he needed extra cash to pay the bills for himself, his wife, and their infant child. "Baseball was clearly my best sport, but I was a decent basketball player, I could run all day and I could rebound," he says. "Problem was I couldn't shoot very well [32 percent from the field, 58 percent from the foul line]. I got lucky, though, and made the team."

At Washington State University, Conley was scouted by virtually every major league club. At 6'8", he was an overpowering right-handed fastball pitcher who led the team to a second-place ranking nationally. In basketball, he was an honorable mention All-America who averaged 20 points a game.

In February of 1950, Conley, only a junior, became a member of the Boston Braves organization after the team offered him a $3,000 signing bonus. That year, he was assigned to Hartford of the Eastern League by the Braves. By August 1, he had a record of 16-3 and was unanimously selected to the All-Star team. Finishing with 20 wins, he became the first Hartford player in history to be named the league's MVP.

In the offseason, Conley, who had gotten married at age 20, decided to supplement his baseball income by playing basketball for the Wilkes-Barre Barons of the struggling American Basketball League. He says, "I played there for one season and then said, 'This is nuts.' All the traveling and practicing was too much for me to handle as a 22-year-old family man. I decided that I'd just concentrate on baseball and tighten up on our budget."

Despite his success on the field, the Conley family, which now included an infant child, was struggling. "I was offered a contract with the Celtics in 1952 and the salary was pretty darn good for a rookie," he says. "As a backup, I played less than 12 minutes a game and averaged better than six rebounds a game. The team was happy with my production, but I wanted to spend more time with my family."

For the next five seasons, Conley concentrated strictly on baseball, earning All-Star honors three times and being the winning pitcher in the 1955 classic. As a member of the Milwaukee Braves in 1957, he helped the team win the World Series over the Yankees, 4-3.

The next year Conley called Red Auerbach and asked for a tryout. "I need a backup for [Bill] Russell, but I really want someone who hasn't been out of the game for six years, I need somebody who can play 10 minutes a game while I rest Russell," the Celtics GM said. "I'll give you a shot, but you're going to have to beat out some pretty good young players, guys who played in the league last year."

By the end of training camp, Auerbach realized Conley was better than any other player he could find. "He's gotten better with time," Red said. "He manages to hold his own against Russ in practice. He's not intimidated one bit. If he can play that way against Russell, he can be effective against anyone."

"Gene knows his limitations," said starting power forward Tommy Heinsohn. "He doesn't look to shoot. He just boxes out, sets picks, out jumps his opponents for rebounds, and runs the court."

Conley's natural position was power forward, yet Auerbach always referred to him as "Russell's backup."

"Being called Russell's backup was a bit embarrassing to me," says Conley. "Hell, Russell played 45 minutes a game. Sure, I played maybe two or three minutes at center, but I was really Heinsohn's backup. I played 10 minutes a game at power forward every game. Still, Red kept calling me Russell's backup, as if Russell and I almost equally shared the minutes at center. It felt awkward when Red mentioned my name with Russell's in the same sentence. Truth is, if Russ and I played a one-on-one game, not only would I have gotten shut out but he would have blocked every shot I attempted."

Fact is, however, Auerbach did use Conley to ease Russell's workload. When the two were on the court at the same time, the Celtics coach used Russell to cover the smaller scoring forwards on the defensive end while Conley, who was thin, no more than 210 pounds, had the unenviable task of guarding the more physical centers such as Chicago's Johnny Red Kerr, Charlie Share, and Detroit's seven-footer Walter Dukes, who used his closed fists and his elbows to pound an opponent in the back to gain position underneath the baskets.

"Basically," says Conley, "my job was to get the crap kicked out of me by blocking out the other team's big men, all of whom outweighed me by at least 20 pounds. But the one thing I did very well was to use my elbows to carve out some space so that Russell could move in and grab all the defensive rebounds."

The Celtics won three straight championships from '59 to '61, with Conley as "Russell's backup," making him the only athlete to win championships in both baseball and basketball. "It was a great experience being a part of those special teams. Today, I don't even mind being called the guy who backed up Bill Russell."

Of course, Boston fans' favorite story about Conley doesn't even involve his time with the Celtics. In fact, he was a Red Sox pitcher when he pulled a stunt that earned him the reputation as a bit of a flake. After a pair of embarrassing losses at Yankee Stadium one weekend in 1962, he and teammate Elijah "Pumpsie" Green, an infielder and the first African American to play for the Sox, got off the team bus and headed to a local bar. Both then had a far too many cocktails at a nightclub. In his drunken state, Conley, who had begun to read the Bible on a daily basis, convinced Green that they ought to take a trip to Israel to visit some of the more famous religious landmarks.

However, they were turned away at airport customs because they didn't have their passports with them. Heading straight to another New York bar, they continued their booze binge, ending up checking in to Waldorf Astoria Hotel. While Green returned to the team the next day, Conley missed a game and did not rejoin the team for two days. During his absence, there were false rumors circulating in the media that he may have been suicidal because of his poor pitching effort against New York.

The attempt to fly to Israel and Conley's subsequent two-day mysterious disappearance resulted in his considering retirement because he was embarrassed by his alcohol-induced actions. However, the Red Sox, after discussing the matter with the pitcher, fined him $2,000 and persuaded him to rejoin the team. Today, the Great Israel Misadventure is still one of baseball's most legendary stories.

Shortly before retiring from baseball in 1963, Gene, now 81, and his wife, Kathryn, bought their own business, the Foxboro Paper Company, which they owned for 35 years. Today they live in Waterville Valley, Maine. The couple, who have been married 58 years, have four children and seven grandchildren.

Where Have You Gone?

MEL COUNTS

The Skyscraper

MEL COUNTS

College: Oregon State | Height: 7'0" | Weight: 230 lbs.
DOB: 10/16/1941 | Position: Center
Years with Celtics: 1964-'65 through 1965-'66

Notes: Two-time All-America selection at Oregon State. Led Beavers to the 1963 Final Four. Member of the 1964 gold medal-winning men's Olympic basketball team. Won two NBA Championships as a member of the Boston Celtics.
Teammate of both Bill Russell and Wilt Chamberlain.

At just a shade over seven feet, Mel Counts covered considerable real estate as he patrolled the Boston Garden paint during the mid-'60s. A one-time backup to Bill Russell, Counts today still thinks in terms of real estate, only now in a very literal sense; the player nicknamed "Goose" is a successful broker for his independently owned Prudential Real Estate franchise.

"I've been a realtor for more than thirty years," says Counts. "Listing and selling properties, investing in properties, things of that nature. It's

81

something that I really enjoy doing. I've been blessed in that regard, no question about it."

Counts has been blessed in many ways; a father of five and grandfather of 14, Counts left basketball following the 1975-'76 NBA season and returned to his native Oregon, where he is very active in his church and also in various civic organizations. A vigorous pro-life supporter, an avid biker, and an expert fisherman, Counts has maintained a positive, fulfilling lifestyle that has left an indelible mark on those who know him. He frequently speaks to church groups and kids groups, and often takes along the gold medal that he won in the 1964 Olympics. He hopes that it inspires others to excel in the endeavors of their choosing, and that it serves as a reminder that, with the right combination of skill and faith, anything is possible.

Indeed. Born on October 16, 1941, in Coos Bay, Oregon, Counts found his inspiration in the small town environment and the natural wonders found only in that part of the country.

"I remember when it rained, you didn't have to worry about your top-side getting wet. It was your bottom-side you had to worry about, because the rain came at you sideways—so an umbrella didn't do you a whole lot of good."

At the time, Coos Bay was the top exporter of lumber in the world. It was also a fishing community, and Counts developed a passion for angling at a very early age. He still hunts and fishes with a lifetime friend from his childhood, and says that his current love—hiking—can be traced directly to his youth. It was a different era, a simpler era, one in which Counts and his friends could safely hitch the three miles from his home to downtown Coos Bay, where he would catch the latest feature in the local movie house before hitching back home in the dark.

With so much to do outdoors, basketball didn't become a real interest until Counts was in the fourth grade. He took to the sport quickly. A natural athlete with good coordination and an innate feel for the game, he worked hard to develop a solid foundation based on the fundamentals.

"One of the best coaches I ever had was my fourth, fifth, and sixth grade coach," he says. "He was a true mentor, and his enthusiasm for the game really helped me to stay interested. He was constantly drilling us with basketball fundamentals. What he did for me then really set the stage for the rest of my life."

Counts went on to become the most accomplished basketball player in the history of Marshfield High School, earning a scholarship to play collegiate hoops for the legendary Slats Gill at Oregon State. Gill, who had guided his 1949 Oregon State team to the Final Four, would do so again in 1963 with Counts as the centerpiece of the team's attack. Counts, then a junior, would earn All-America honors for his efforts, a feat that he would repeat following his senior season.

"To me, Slats was one of the greatest college coaches ever," says Counts. "To have the opportunity to play in the Final Four was something special. I think that nine of the 13 players were from Oregon. Terry Baker was on that team—he had won the Heisman Trophy and was also the *Sports Illustrated* Sportsman of the Year. Steve Pauley was a decathlon champion. We had two or three baseball players. We didn't have the best record of any Oregon State team, but we had a real cohesive group and we came together at the right time. We made it to the Final Four, lost to Cincinnati, and then lost to Duke in the consolation game. Back then you played two games regardless. It was just a special time and a wonderful experience to have. To represent the state of Oregon was quite a privilege and quite an honor."

The 1964 Olympic Games were held in Tokyo, and Counts was selected to play for the legendary Hank Iba. As hard as it may be to fathom, the U.S. men's basketball team was considered something of an underdog going into the 18th Olympiad. The Soviet Union had made great strides with its basketball program. The world, it seemed, was catching up.

"The writers wrote us off," he says, still perturbed by the sleight after all of these years. "They said that we weren't going to get the job done. We didn't have a Jerry West, or an Oscar Robertson, or a Walt Bellamy. These guys went on to become superstars in the NBA. We didn't have anybody on our team like that. But we did have Hank Iba and a great group of assistant coaches.

"We went to Pearl Harbor and worked out for three weeks. We worked out twice a day, for three hours a pop, and when it came game time we were ready. We were extremely well-prepared and extremely well-conditioned. We went in with confidence, tradition, and the idea that the sports writers had written us off. Our goal was to represent our country to the best of our ability, and that's exactly what we did. We won the gold medal and proved everybody wrong."

The Boston Celtics selected Counts in the first round of the 1964 NBA Draft, the ninth player chosen overall. He arrived in the best shape of his life. He had heard the horror stories of Red Auerbach's training camps, and of how the Celtics were annually the best-conditioned players in the league. Following those grueling practices at Pearl Harbor, he felt more than ready to hold his own.

"That first Celtics training camp felt like boot camp," Counts says, smiling. "The first three days we didn't shoot the basketball. In fact, back then they didn't know as much about nutrition as they know now, and about how the body recovers from exercise. We'd go full-bore from 10 until 12, and then from two until four, with hardly a drink of water. There wouldn't be any breaks. Now they practice in the morning and in the evening, which makes more sense. It gives the body more time to recover.

"But the fact that they ran so much in training camp certainly gave the Celtics an edge. Having Bill Russell, the greatest defensive player in the history of the game, didn't hurt, either. It all played into Red's up-tempo offense, which was predicated on the fast break. Those training camps were quite an experience."

The Celtics won a seventh consecutive championship during Counts's rookie campaign. The season was noteworthy for two other reasons as well: team founder Walter Brown's passing on September 7 and John Havlicek's legendary steal during the 1965 Eastern Conference Finals.

"The guide wire supporting the backboard almost cost us that game against the Sixers," Counts says. "I remember a conversation between Red Auerbach and Bill Russell prior to that series, and the decision was made to leave the guide wire in place. Well, it was a really close game and Russell had to inbound the basketball. Sure enough, he hit that wire and gave the ball back to Philadelphia under their basket. I thought, 'Oh no, this is it,' and then Havlicek came out of nowhere to steal the basketball. He was a smart, smart player. He grabbed the ball, made the pass to Sam Jones, and the rest is history."

The Celtics won their seventh consecutive a series later. For Counts, it was his first championship at any level.

"At the time you don't really take it all in," he says, "but as time goes on it becomes more meaningful. Now I can look at my Celtic ring or my Celtic watch, and say 'Hey, I was on a world championship team.' I've been very blessed and very fortunate to play on those teams."

The Celtics would win it all again a year later. Counts was then traded to Baltimore for versatile forward Bailey Howell, who would go on to win a pair of titles of his own. The stay in Baltimore was short-lived, however, as Counts soon found himself headed to the Lakers. Suddenly, he found himself playing on the other side of the NBA's most intense rivalry.

"It was great. I had the opportunity to be in a championship situation with the Celtics, and I wanted to accomplish the same thing with the Lakers. It was also special because I had the pleasure of playing with the two greatest centers in the history of the NBA—Bill Russell and Wilt Chamberlain. So it was a very satisfying experience."

These days, Counts still shares his basketball experiences with others. The Celtics remain a very big part of who he is, even though he spent just two of his 12 seasons with the team. He won his only championships there, and he teamed with some of the greatest players ever, during arguably the greatest dynasty in the history of professional sports. His has been the good life, and he knows it.

"I've been blessed," he says. "How many people can say that they've played with guys like Russell, Havlicek, Sam Jones, Tommy Heinsohn, K. C. Jones, and Satch Sanders? I'm extremely lucky in that regard, and I've got the rings to prove it."

TERRY DUEROD

Doing the "D-O-O-O-O"

TERRY DUEROD

College: University of Detroit | Height: 6'2" | Weight: 180 lbs.
DOB: 07/29/1956 | Position: Guard
Years with Celtics: 1980-'81, 1981-'82

Notes: Drafted by the Detroit Pistons in the third round of 1979 draft.
Signed as a free agent by the Boston Celtics on December 4, 1980.
Waived by Boston on October 26, 1982.

His signing rated nothing more than a sentence in the transactions column. In fact, when Boston signed Terry Duerod to a 10-day contract in December of 1980, the second-year NBA guard knew he might not stick around long enough to have time to unpack his suitcase. After all, the Celtics had a deep backcourt corps, including Tiny Archibald, Gerald Henderson, Chris Ford, and M. L. Carr.

A third-round pick of the Pistons in 1979, Duerod had an outstanding college career at the University of Detroit where he averaged 23.3 points on 53 percent shooting as a senior. In his first NBA season with Detroit, Duerod played solidly, scoring 9.3 points per game on 47 percent accuracy. After being selected by Dallas in the 1980 expansion draft, Duerod was shocked when he was cut just two months into the season.

"I was getting decent [playing] time," recalls Duerod. "My shooting touch was good, and I was fifth on the team in scoring. Next thing I know, they call me in after a practice to tell me they had released me. No one explained why."

Fortunately for Duerod, the Celtics brass, particularly Bill Fitch, liked the 23-year-old's shooter's mentality. As soon as he cleared waivers, Boston signed him. "When I arrived, the first thing Coach told me was that he brought me in because he knew I hit the outside shot," says Duerod. "Basically, he let me know that if I was open and got the ball, he didn't want me to hesitate.

"That talk made me feel pretty good about my chances of sticking. I was realistic, though. I was on a great team. I was the fifth guard, just a second-year guy on a 10-day. No one had to tell me the minutes weren't going to come easy."

Duerod made his Celtics debut in the closing minute of his third game in uniform against the Knicks at Madison Square Garden. On a fast break, his lone field goal try, a jumper from the top of the key, rimmed out.

"About the only thing I remember," he says, "was what Larry Bird said to me afterward in the locker room. He told me to take that shot every time."

In the next game, a Boston blowout over Indiana at the Garden, Fitch called on Duerod in the fourth quarter. Once again, the eager-to-please guard found himself wide open, this time from beyond the three-point arc. This time he didn't miss. The sellout crowd acknowledged his basket with a burst of applause while the now-resting Celtic starters stood up and yelled out words of encouragement.

After the game, Fitch informed Duerod that the Celtics were going to sign him to a second 10-day contract. In his next few appearances, the long-distance shooter played well enough to convince Red Auerbach to offer him a contract for the remainder of the season.

It was in mid-January when Duerod put on a garbage-time shooting exhibition against the Nets that would endear him to the Garden crowd for as long as he wore a Celtics uniform. With less than four minutes remaining and Boston safely in front, Fitch looked down toward the end of the bench and motioned for the guard to sub in. Sprinting to the scorer's table, Duerod smiled as several courtside spectators shouted out, "D-O-O-O-O." Not more than a minute after entering the game, Duerod came off a pick and buried a mid-range jumper. Two possessions later, he took a pass and flicked in a baseline pull-up. The deep-voiced sounds of "D-O-O-O-O" were now becoming much louder. And when he effortlessly dropped in a 20-footer for his third straight basket, the whole building was doing the "D-O-O-O-O."

On the Celtics bench, M. L. Carr realized he might be witnessing the birth of a folk hero. "Max, Larry, Chris, myself, we were all standing, waving our arms, and looking up at the crowd," he says. "I mean people were having so much fun. I still remember Larry pointing at Terry and yelling for our guys on the court to get him the ball. And to cap everything off, he got wide open for a three-pointer and nailed it. We're all high-fiving each other and going, 'D-O-O-O-O, D-O-O-O-O, D-O-O-O-O.'"

When the final buzzer sounded, the somewhat startled reserve headed toward midcourt where most of his teammates formed a spontaneous welcoming line. Hundreds of fans were still at their seats, serenading Duerod with rhythmic chants as he headed to the locker room.

"I guess I was smiling, I don't remember. It was like being in the Twilight Zone," he says. "I couldn't believe how the crowd had reacted. I mean it was just garbage time. . . . To see and hear everyone cheering for me like that, it was unbelievable, something I'll never forget."

Although Duerod averaged only 2.5 points for the Celtics during the 1980-'81 regular season, fans never failed to salute him when he made his usual late fourth-quarter appearances. "He was the exact type of guy Fitch looked for in an 11th or 12th man, someone who was hard-working, knew his role, and got along with everybody," says Gerald Henderson. "Don't get me wrong, Terry had talent and wanted to play as much as anyone, but if he didn't get in, he didn't complain. He'd just keep going all out in practice, staying late to play in our subs versus starters three-on-three or four-on-four games, getting ready for the next game."

Of course, Duerod's proudest moment came when the Celtics captured their 14th world championship by beating the Rockets, 4-2 in the 1981 NBA finals. "Being a part of that team, getting my ring, those are memories I always think about."

In the 1981 draft, the Celtics picked Wyoming's Charles Bradley, a 6'5" guard, in the first round and then took a calculated gamble in the third round by selecting Toronto Blue Jays utility player Danny Ainge, BYU's Wooden Award-winning backcourt star. It appeared Duerod's chance of earning a spot on the Boston roster was nil. However, it took Ainge until early December to resolve a legal battle with Toronto to free him from his baseball obligations and sign with Boston.

"Honestly, when I went to training camp, I expected to be released as soon as Boston was able to sign Danny. The Celtics obviously wanted some size at shooting guard. Charles and Danny were both draft picks.

They were going to get guaranteed contracts. They both were three inches taller than me," he says. "Still, I had learned that anything is possible when I got cut by an expansion team and picked up by a team that won an NBA title."

Duerod, with his determination and enthusiasm, not only made the club, he was kept as insurance by Fitch even after Ainge joined the team. For the final four months of the season, he was "stashed" on injured reserve. "I understood the situation. I would have loved to have been playing instead of watching, but. . ." he says, with a knowing smile.

Cut by the Celtics shortly before the start of the 1982-'83 season, Duerod was signed by the Warriors but played only five games before he was released. It was his last NBA stop. He spent a year with the Detroit Spirits of the CBA and then played for Scavolini in the Italian League. He finished his pro career in the Philippines, where he played two years.

"After that, my wife, Rosemary, and I decided to go back to Detroit," Duerod says. "I enjoyed being overseas, but all the travel and cultural differences get to you. It was just time to settle down."

Not surprisingly, Duerod found a challenging and rewarding job, becoming a Detroit firefighter in 1987.

"I'm an engineer," he says proudly. "My job is to drive the truck and then to control the water pressure once we arrive at a fire. I've been in some tough situations, like the time we arrived at an apartment fire and saw people jumping out of windows to escape the flames. You have to react so quickly. There's pressure because our job is to save people's lives and protect their property. It's been a job I loved from the day I started."

At 50, Duerod still plays in the Detroit firefighters basketball league. "My knees are a little worn out, but I still enjoy the competition," he says. "As long as my shot is still going in, I'll manage to gimp my way up and down the court."

Where Have You Gone?

WAYNE EMBRY

Central Character

WAYNE EMBRY

College: Miami (OH) | Height: 6'8" | Weight: 255 lbs.
DOB: 03/26/1937 | Position: Center
Years with Celtics: 1966-'67, 1967-'68

Notes: Honorable Mention All-America at Miami (1957, 1958). Five-time consecutive NBA All-Star (1961-'65). Captain, Cincinnati Royals (1962-'66). NBA championship with Boston Celtics (1968). First captain, Milwaukee Bucks (1968-'69). First African American NBA General Manager, Milwaukee Bucks (1971-'79). First African American NBA Team President and Chief Operating Officer, Cleveland Cavaliers (1994). The *Sporting News* NBA Executive of the Year (1992, 1998). Inducted into the Naismith Memorial Basketball Hall of Fame as a contributor on October 1, 1999.

Johnny Most nicknamed him "The Wall," a tribute to the bone-rattling picks that he set as a member of the Boston Celtics, and today his considerable influence stretches from the NBA to Wall Street and back again. Wayne Embry's latest foray into professional basketball is with the Toronto Raptors, where he serves as Senior Basketball Advisor to the President. Embry joined the Raptors organization in June 2004 as Senior

Advisor to the General Manager, and in 2006 also served briefly as the team's interim General Manager. Now at age 74, Embry shows no signs of slowing down. His eyes, it seems, are fixed squarely on building a championship contender.

"You always face issues when you are trying to build a team," Embry says flatly. "It is no different here. In terms of what I bring to the table and the things that I can do to have an impact on an organization and help to make it successful, well, I feel that my track record as an executive speaks for itself. I have been involved with the Toronto Raptors since 2004, and I just hope that I can play an integral part in this team's continued transformation and success. Anyone who knows me knows that I hate to lose. I have a passion for winning, so hopefully my involvement will contribute toward the goal of winning a championship."

The man knows his hoops, no question about that. But spend a few minutes talking to Wayne Embry, and it isn't long before you realize that this former NBA All-Star is far more than a link to the days when legends such as Russell and Chamberlain ruled the basketball universe. Embry is as relevant now as he was then, only in areas that extend far beyond the hardwood. Backboards have morphed into boardrooms. Bone-crunching picks have given way to civic stewardship. From trading elbows with Willis Reed to rubbing elbows with former Federal Reserve Chairman Alan Greenspan, Embry is the rare athlete who has eclipsed his own star power in terms of off-the-court accomplishments.

Alan Greenspan?

"I served as a member of the Board of Directors for the Bank of Cleveland, but didn't interact directly with Greenspan," Embry replies when the subject returns to the former Fed chief. "The Bank of Cleveland reports to the Central Bank, which plays a large role in shaping monetary and economic policy. My time on the board was very educational. It was interesting work, and very rewarding. So while I wasn't directly involved with Greenspan, I was still able to have an important voice within the Bank of Cleveland."

And what was it like to serve in such a prestigious and powerful capacity?

"The primary responsibilities of directors range from the supervision of the Federal Reserve Bank of Cleveland's operations, to making recommendations on the Bank's discount rate. Directors appoint the Reserve Bank's president and the first vice president, which is subject to approval by the Board of Governors. Directors also review their Reserve Bank's budget and expenditures. They're also responsible for the internal audit program of the Bank. The Federal Reserve Act also requires directors to set the Bank's discount rate every two weeks, which is also subject to approval by the Board of Governors. It was an honor to serve and to be involved. It was a privilege to sit on the board."

Clearly, Embry's management skills have served him well as an NBA executive, business owner, and board member. His résumé includes that impressive five-year term with the Federal Reserve Bank. He has his ongoing gig with the Raptors. And he has been a pioneer in terms of breaking the NBA front office color barrier—Embry became the NBA's first African American general manager in 1972, and in 1994 was named the first African American NBA team president and chief operating officer.

"I was the GM in Milwaukee for eight seasons," he says. "I began working in the front office in 1971. The owners knew that I had a close relationship with Oscar Robertson, so they asked me to make a call on their behalf. I made the key inquiry for them. Having Kareem [then Lew Alcindor] and Oscar on the same team was an unbelievable combination for us. We won the championship that year, and the next season I was promoted to general manager."

Embry's relationship with Robertson dated back to their playing days in Cincinnati. The two men remain close, and speak often by telephone.

"Oscar, in my opinion, is the best to ever play the game of basketball. We were roommates when I was with the Royals, and it was an honor to be on the same team with him. He certainly enhanced my career. He had a great impact on me, but his influence extended beyond basketball and into the bigger picture of life. As you can tell, I have a tremendous amount of respect and admiration for the man."

Born and raised in Ohio, Embry began his basketball career at Tecumseh High School before starring at Miami of Ohio, where he was a two-time honorable mention All-America selection, and where his number has long since been retired. Back then, Embry stayed in school the entire four years; in his new role with the Raptors, he sees an entirely different landscape.

Embry says, "Well, today you see teenagers jumping to the pros after one season of college ball, which is something that just didn't happen when I played. You have to factor that into the decision-making process. Even if that had been the trend during my era, I simply wasn't prepared to play professional basketball. College was the best route for me. I was a somewhat of a slow developer—as a freshman I wasn't even the best player on the team—but by my sophomore season I'd improved in every aspect of my game and had much greater confidence in my ability. I blossomed during my junior year, and things really took off from that point on."

As a pro, Embry was a five-time All-Star for the Cincinnati Royals, playing alongside such legendary stars as the Big O (Robertson) and Jerry Lucas. An NBA championship proved elusive, however, as the Royals routinely failed to supplant the Boston Celtics as kings of the East. In a classic case of "If you can't beat 'em, join 'em," Red Auerbach acquired Embry in 1966 as a backup to the incomparable Bill Russell. After being dethroned by Chamberlain and the Philadelphia 76ers in 1967, the Celtics—with Embry—were back on top, winning a league-best 10 NBA championships.

"There was a great sense of relief," he says. "After playing the game for so long, and after being frustrated by Russell and the Celtics all of those years, it was just a great relief to finally be able to win a championship."

And what about that nickname?

"Johnny Most was the one who gave me that nickname. He liked the way I set picks [laughs]."

Embry's natural proclivity towards management left him in awe of legendary coach Red Auerbach. Often referred to as a genius, Auerbach's approach to the game—especially the way he handled players of all stature and accomplishment—intrigued the aspiring front office executive.

"Red had a tremendous management style," says Embry. "It was at the foundation of his success as a coach and general manager. You look at the way he motivated players and you begin to understand the man's talent. He instinctively knew that some guys would respond to screaming, while others responded better to criticism behind closed doors. So the way he managed a Tom Heinsohn was completely different from the way he managed a Bob Cousy or a Bill Russell. There is a lot to say for that. I adopted and emulated that style in both sports and business, and it has worked well for me."

And then there is Russell. Did Embry learn anything from the man who won on every level imaginable?

"Russell was the greatest competitor and the greatest winner in the history of professional sports. The Celtics won 11 championships during his 13 years with the team, which, in my mind, ranks as the greatest dynasty ever. The New York Yankees may have won more championships, but those are spread out over decades. To win 11 titles in 13 years is an incredible accomplishment.

"I learned a lot from being around Russell, and immersing myself in the championship culture that he was responsible for developing there. He was once asked about winning and said, 'If you have to play, you might as well win.' When you think about things in those terms, then you can't help but expect more out of yourself. As an executive practicing management skills, I find those are valuable words to live by."

In 1985, Embry's management skills would be put to the ultimate test. The moribund Cleveland Cavaliers, mired in a losing funk that threatened the very existence of the franchise, hired Embry to reverse the fortunes of the basketball faithful in Northern Ohio. Under his direction as vice-president and general manager, the Cavaliers won 40 or more games 10 times, 50 or more on three occasions, and advanced to the Eastern Conference Finals in 1992.

"Turning the Cavaliers into a winner was an awesome challenge," he says, "but it was well worth it. Like I said, winning is very important to me. To help the franchise overcome years of underachieving and mismanagement is something of which I can be proud."

Embry was promoted to executive vice-president position with the club in 1992. Two seasons later he broke the NBA's color barrier once again, becoming the first African American NBA team president and chief operating officer. Recognition for his work with the Cavs was never far away: Embry earned the *Sporting News* Executive of the Year honor in 1992 and 1998, as well as the *Sports Illustrated* Executive of the Year award in 1998.

"It's nice to be recognized," says Embry. "But more than that, it's also very rewarding to see all of your hard work pay off. When you look at where the Cleveland franchise was when I took over, and where it was when I left, that's really the most important thing. The Cavaliers were a much more viable product at the end of my stay."

The ultimate recognition came on October 1, 1999, when Embry was inducted into the Naismith Memorial Basketball Hall of Fame—not as a player, despite the All-America honors, All-Star appearances, and world championship ring, but as a contributor known for his shrewd moves and winning management style.

"Being honored in that way was something I never dreamed of, and it makes you realize that not many people get that kind of recognition. My goal was simply to do a good job. Obviously, I'm very honored to be included in such an elite group who have already been enshrined into the Hall of Fame. I'm pleased and I feel privileged to be part of that group. It was definitely the highlight of my career."

Now the man known as "The Wall" has put the accolades on hold and continues to embrace the challenge of building a championship contender in Toronto. And if history is any indication, the Raptors will be much better off because of it.

"I'm here to advise on all things related to basketball and basketball operations," Embry says. "I have more than 50 years of experience and expertise, and I enjoy contributing in ways small and large. We have a solid management team in place, and the organization is headed in the right direction."

HANK FINKEL

"High Henry"

HANK FINKEL

College: University of Dayton | Height: 7'0"
Weight: 245 lbs. | DOB: 04/20/1942 | Position: Center
Years with Celtics: 1969 through '75

Notes: Sold by the San Diego Clippers to the Celtics for cash and a draft choice on August 22, 1969. Member of Celtics' 1974 championship team.

He was the man who replaced the retired Bill Russell in the Celtics' starting lineup. Of course, for Henry Finkel, it was the ultimate "can't-win" situation.

Despite an abundance of desire and hustle, the seven-foot University of Dayton product just didn't possess one-tenth of Russell's quickness and skills, or his instinctive knack for playing the game. And the Boston Garden fans were not at all pleased when massive muscular giants such as Wilt Chamberlain, Willis Reed, Walt Bellamy, and Wes Unseld bullied their way to the basket as Boston's center attempted to simply hold his defensive position in the paint and limit his opponents' production.

Rookie Celtics head coach Tom Heinsohn experimented with different frontcourt lineups, using Finkel at both center and power forward, usually as a starter, although he also was occasionally brought in as the sixth man. But without Russell and Sam Jones, who had also retired, the 1969-'70 Celtics struggled throughout the season and finished out of the playoffs for the first time since 1950, with a record of 34-48.

Finkel was Public Enemy No. 1, as the fans showered him with choruses of boos, mixed with occasional derogatory comments. No one was more upset with the crowd's behavior than Heinsohn.

"No reporter has ever heard one word out of my mouth about Henry Finkel's effort," Heinsohn said after one loss in which Finkel was the constant target of crowd critics. "Hank's come in here and has been a total professional. I think our fans should be supportive, not negative. Henry Finkel is not the reason we're losing. It's not fair for him to be singled out as the symbol for this team's problems. You lose a Bill Russell, and there are going to be consequences. We'll get better; it just won't happen overnight."

Finkel, who led the nation in field goal percentage as a senior in college, was selected in the fourth round of the 1966 draft by the Lakers and played 27 games as a rookie, with such greats as Elgin Baylor, Jerry West, and Gail Goodrich as teammates. Chosen by San Diego in the 1967 expansion draft, Finkel then spent two seasons on the West Coast before being traded to Boston.

"People said I was acquired to be Russell's replacement," says Finkel, who split the starting center responsibilities with 6'9" Rich Johnson. "That bothered me because everyone knew no one in the NBA could 'replace' Bill Russell. Heck, I was just an average reserve player. Before I even put on the Celtics uniform, I knew I wasn't a legitimate starting center in this league. I didn't kid myself. I didn't have great talent, so I just made up my mind to try and outwork whoever was matched up against me. But the Boston fans, at least during my first year as a Celtic, had some unrealistic expectations about my abilities. I knew I wasn't capable of playing at the level they thought I could."

The season took its toll on Finkel, who never complained about the unfair treatment he had received at the Garden. "I have to admit I thought about retiring," he says. "It wasn't an easy year. I'd come home after a game and just feel totally drained and depressed. The money I was making wasn't that great, so I thought I might move to San Diego, where I had some good business contacts from when I played there. Fortunately, Red Auerbach, Tommy, and a few of my close teammates talked me out of it."

To his credit, Finkel gradually won over fans with his humble, friendly personality. The fact that he was always willing to sign autographs and take the time to talk with fans enabled him to go from goat to fan favorite in a year's time.

"At seven feet, I was hard to miss," he says. "Thanks to Johnny Most, who gave me the nickname 'High Henry,' people would come up to me and just want to say hello and tell me they were rooting for me. It was flattering, and I enjoyed just talking basketball with the fans because they cared so much about the Celtics."

Boston drafted Dave Cowens and obtained power forward Paul Silas, a rebounding machine, in the offseason following Finkel's first year as a Celtic.

"Tommy used me to back up Dave and even Paul at times," recalls Finkel. "The key thing is that I was almost always playing next to an All Star who could score and rebound. I'd block out on the boards, set picks, and occasionally roll to the basket for an easy layup. Basketball was fun again."

The thought of retirement vanished from Finkel's mind, and he thoroughly enjoyed his new role as a reserve.

"I like to think I was a team player who knew the game. I knew I wasn't going to out jump too many guys, so I would try to always get good rebounding position and then box guys out," the gangly, wide-shouldered Finkel says. "On offense, I'd take the open shot because I had a decent jumper, but the thing I did best was set picks for our scorers, especially for John Havlicek. John and I worked well together. I remember one game in Buffalo where I was standing in the frontcourt and John had just gotten a defensive rebound. [Braves guard] Randy Smith, one of the fastest players in the league, started chasing John. Havlicek saw me sticking out my butt to set a pick and took off towards me at full speed. Well, Randy Smith never saw what was coming, and he just crumbled when he ran into me. That left John with an easy jumper for an uncontested basket.

"In the NBA, if you can set a pick that frees guys like Havlicek, [Don] Nelson, [Paul] Westphal, or [Jo Jo] White for just a quarter of a second, they will come off the screen and hit 70 percent of those shots. My job was to give them that split second to free them up for a jumper. I took pride in doing all the little things for the team, which made the job of our All Star players a little easier."

Following the 1974-'75 season, his sixth year as a Celtic, "High Henry" decided to retire. "Of course winning the '74 championship was the highlight of my career," he says. "Truthfully, though, the greatest thrill of my years with Boston was just enjoying the tremendous camaraderie. I made so many great friends. The guys I played with, from the starters to the reserves, were all so unselfish, so special. I don't think any team was as close as we were."

Finkel planned on moving his family to San Diego until Jerry Volk, Jan Volk's father, called with a job offer. Jerry Volk was opening a new business and thought the popular Finkel, with his easy-going, straightforward personality would make an excellent salesman.

"Things were going well for me financially and personally," says Finkel. "Then, one night at a Celtics game I was told that Jerry had passed away suddenly. The man had always treated me so well. I knew things wouldn't be the same without him as my boss, so I eventually quit.

"My degree from Dayton was in education, so I thought about becoming a teacher. Revere High School offered me the varsity basketball coaching job, but they didn't have a teaching opening. Then I received an offer to coach at Robert Morris University, just outside Pittsburgh. By then, my family just loved living in the Boston area so much, I couldn't bring myself to relocate. My old teammate, Don Nelson, who was coaching the Bucks, offered me a chance to scout part-time for him, but I really wanted a job that would allow me to spend time at home. In the end, I opened up my own office furniture sales company. I've stayed with it for almost 29 years now, and it's been very rewarding."

Finkel resides in Lynnfield, Massachusetts, with his wife, Kathleen. The couple has two children, Dennis and Wendy, and three grandchildren. "Even today, I'll be in a local store or just walking down the street and someone will yell out, 'Hey, High Henry, how ya doing?' I never get tired of it. I'm 70 now, so it's a nice feeling to be remembered after all these years."

Where Have You Gone?

KEVIN GAMBLE

Hang Time

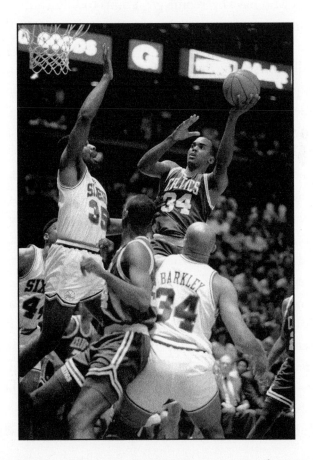

KEVIN GAMBLE

College: Iowa | Height: 6'5"
Weight: 210 lbs. | DOB: 11/13/1965 | Position: Guard
Years with Celtics: 1988-'89 through 1993-'94

Notes: Led Lanphier High in Springfield, Illinois, to a state championship in 1983. As a senior at Iowa, led the Hawkeyes to a 30-5 record and the NCAA tournament regional finals. Selected by Portland in the third round of the 1987 NBA Draft. Played two seasons in the CBA before getting a call by the Boston Celtics. Excellent play at end of '88-'89 season (subbing for an injured Dennis Johnson) led to long-term contract with Celtics.

The sports world has no shortage of Hollywood-style success stories, of players who have overcome great odds to fulfill a dream, overcome tragedy, or capture the imaginations of millions. The 1980 U.S. Olympic Hockey Team shocks the world, and just like that we believe in miracles. Rudy doggedly pursues a shot at Notre Dame football, and the movie ends with the 5-foot-nothin', 100-and-nothin' pound dreamer being carried off the field on the shoulders of All-Americans. At the other end of the spectrum are the truly elite, the athletes whose skill and charisma transcend their sport and cross over into popular culture—think Babe Ruth, Muhammad Ali, and Tiger Woods. We're on a one-name basis with these superstars, legends who will be known for generations to come. Lost in-between are the stories of those athletes who simply hang in there and never give up. They persevere, refusing to be cast aside, insisting that their talent is good enough to share the stage with the greatest athletes in the world—this even when logic and common sense dictate otherwise.

Kevin Gamble knows what it's like to persevere. The one-time high school standout took a circuitous route to the Boston Celtics and the NBA, playing basketball at both the junior college level and Division I levels before taking his dream to the CBA and, eventually, to the Philippines and back again. He never doubted himself, convinced that he was capable of not only reaching the NBA, but also of forging a long, successful career at the game's highest level. Today the multi-faceted Gamble is still in love with the game, having served as head coach at the University of Illinois at Springfield for eight seasons before taking a post at Providence of the Big East Conference and, most recently, teaming with fellow Lanphier High alum and current Philadelphia 76er Andre Iguodala to host the 2011 Iguodala and Gamble Basketball Camp in Gamble's hometown of Springfield.

"Basketball is in my blood," Gamble says, reflecting on his post-NBA coaching career. "I was lucky to be the head coach at the University of Illinois Springfield for eight seasons, and there were a lot of great memories of my time there. It was a great experience, and it was a very unique and challenging opportunity because we were able to basically build the program from the ground up. Leaving for the Providence job was bittersweet, because I was the first UIS basketball coach."

From the ground up is exactly how Gamble built his NBA career, one proverbial brick at a time. A star at Springfield's Lanphier High, Gamble led Lions to a state championship in 1983. Even then, success was the result of years of preparation.

"We knew we were going to have a pretty good ball club when we were seniors in high school," he says. "We had the same players that we had in the eighth and ninth grade, so it was a good nucleus of players. A state championship was something that was always in our minds, and we were fortunate enough to go out and get the job done."

Few questioned Gamble's ability at the high school level, but many college recruiters wondered whether he had Division I potential. Undeterred, Gamble enrolled at Lincoln Junior College following graduation, where he played for two seasons under the guidance and tutelage of head coach Alan Pickering.

"Growing up, my parents were very important to me and I looked up to them in many ways. The thing I remember about Coach Pick was of him being the first role model of my adult life. He helped to mold me, and helped to show me what I needed to do to make it at the college level. He taught me how to be a better basketball player, which I appreciate greatly, but more than that he helped me to become a man."

Pickering's basketball influence on Gamble could be summed up in one word: defense. The wise coach knew that his star pupil could produce on offense, but he also knew that Gamble's ticket to Division I basketball rested with his commitment to playing tenacious D. Gamble soaked in the many lessons learned during those two seasons at Lincoln, and a year later found himself playing basketball for the University of Iowa. Head coach George Raveling, however, wasn't overly-impressed by what he saw. Gamble's first year in Iowa City was spent mostly on the bench, watching the action and wondering if his time would ever come, as player and coach failed to see eye-to-eye on nearly everything related to basketball.

As if by divine intervention, Tom Davis replaced Raveling at season's end. Gamble responded in a big way. Suddenly the focal point of the offense, he led the Hawkeyes to a 30-5 record and the NCAA tournament regional finals.

"It was a great experience being part of a great university like Iowa. My first year was fun off the court, but on the court it was very disappointing. Not that Coach Raveling and I didn't get along; it was just that he didn't see me as the player that Coach Pick saw me as, or the player that my high school coach saw me as. At Lanphier I played shooting guard and small forward, and at Lincoln I was primarily a shooting guard. But once I got to Iowa, Coach Raveling saw fit to play me at power forward with guys like Ed Horton and Brad Lohaus. Much bigger guys than I was, both in height and weight. I wish I could have red shirted, because I averaged a total of six minutes per game that year.

"Thankfully, Coach Davis came in that next year and started everyone off with a clean slate. He told us that nobody had positions, and that everyone on the team had to earn their playing time. I practiced hard and won two positions—the two guard and small forward spot—but ended up mostly playing the two. Coach Davis is probably the main reason that I made it to the NBA. Because of him I had a pretty good senior season, and a pretty good tournament, and ended up being drafted by the Portland Trail Blazers in the third round."

Gamble's stay in Portland was brief—nine games in total—before being waived and forced to persevere yet again. When he left the Blazers, he also left convinced that he could compete in the NBA. Battling players such as Clyde Drexler and Terry Porter in training camp helped. Grasping the offensive and defensive schemes as rapidly as he did also was a plus. But understanding that he'd been caught up in a numbers game may have been the biggest boost of all.

"They had some guys on the injured list," Gamble says matter-of-factly. "John Paxson and Ronnie Murphy were the key guys out with injuries. Paxson was an established veteran, and Murphy was the team's first round draft choice. So I knew that the team would make some changes when these guys were healthy enough to play."

Gamble went to the Pistons camp the following summer, only to find himself in a situation eerily similar to that in Portland. The CBA was the next obvious avenue. Gamble took it without hesitation.

"I just kept plugging away. I played a full CBA season, where I played pretty well—I think I averaged 20 points and 10 rebounds—and everyone there stressed that I had to play defense to make it to the NBA. So that's what I worked on."

The Milwaukee Bucks invited him to their camp prior to the start of the 1988-'89 season. Released just two weeks later, he played in the Philippines for a month, returned to the CBA for a 12-game stint with Quad Cities, before receiving a call from the Boston Celtics. This time Gamble was ready.

"I played twelve games for Quad Cities," he says, "and I was averaging close to 30 points a game. That's when I got the call from the Boston Celtics."

An injury to Larry Bird gave Gamble his chance. He was determined to stick. Still, he knew that it would not be easy; the roster was populated with Hall-of-Fame talent, legendary players like Bird, Kevin McHale, and Robert Parish, as well as key contributors such as Dennis Johnson, Danny Ainge, and Brian Shaw. Gamble logged 17 "DNP—Coaches Decisions" that first year, and it looked like the team would make him available in the expansion draft to either Orlando or Minnesota. But then he turned in seven strong minutes in a road win over Philadelphia. He followed that by playing exceptionally well in place of an injured Dennis Johnson the final six games of the regular season.

"It was exciting for me," Gamble says. "Ironically, it was another injury that provided my opportunity to play. DJ rolled his ankle in Atlanta—everyone knew that it was really bad. We didn't know if he was going to miss the last six games, but we knew the next game was out of the question. The next game was against Cleveland. Coach [Jimmy] Rodgers comes into the locker room, goes over the pre-game talk, and tells us who the Cavaliers are starting. He tells us that they're starting Larry Nance, Brad Daugherty, Ron Harper . . . he tells Brian Shaw that he's guarding Mark Price, and then he tells me that I'm guarding Harper. That was the first time that I heard that I was going to be starting an NBA ball game. Of course everybody knows Ron. He's known for his offensive and defensive play. It was exciting but nerve-wracking. Somehow I had a terrific game. I had something like 20 points, 10 assists, and seven rebounds."

By the following season Gamble was firmly established as an integral part of the Boston Celtics. It was a time of transition for the team, as the Big Three of Bird, Parish and McHale were starting to decline, and young players such as Shaw and Reggie Lewis were being groomed for future greatness. Gamble would go on to play five full seasons for the Celtics before retiring with Miami in '96.

"I'll always be a Boston Celtic," Gamble says. "There were so many great times. I remember signing my first big contract with the team—Red just couldn't understand how a guy who couldn't rebound could command a million dollar contract. I remember that before the games, Red would come into the locker room and talk about the days when he coached. The guys would be trying to get their ankles taped, and Red would be sitting on the trainer's table, telling his stories . . . the time would be ticking, and you're trying to get ready to play. But those were special times. For Red to take the time to talk to you, it showed you how much he cared about us as players."

Gamble continues to persevere, earning his stripes as a basketball coach the same way he earned them as a player. He knows that there aren't any shortcuts in life, and that success only comes through hard work and determination. In June, 2010, Gamble walked away from his UIS coaching gig to take a position on Coach Keno Davis's staff at Providence College.

Keno, the son of Gamble's coach at Iowa, offered Gamble the position of Coordinator of Player Development. Gamble, who has always dreamed of coaching at the Division I level, jumped at the opportunity.

"It was like being a fourth assistant coach on his staff," Gamble says. "It wasn't a hard transition to make. I have roots in New England after playing in Boston. My wife is from Boston. It was a great opportunity and it was definitely worth the risk."

The coaching stint with the Friars would last only one season, because Keno Davis was fired on March 28, 2011, following three seasons at the Providence, Rhode Island, school. Ed Cooley was hired shortly thereafter. Cooley cleaned house, and Gamble suddenly found himself looking for a job.

"That's just part of the business," Gamble says. "You just pick yourself up and you persevere."

Gamble attended the 2011 NCAA Final Four, networking with other coaches and setting the stage for the next chapter in a remarkable basketball career. He also teamed with Iguodala to host their basketball camp for a second straight year. In addition, he involved himself with the North Shore Bobcats, serving as a coach for the 16-under boys AAU team in nearby Peabody, Massachusetts.

"I love basketball," Gamble says. "There will be another coaching opportunity out there for me. Sooner or later I'll find it."

If his remarkable playing career is any indication, Kevin Gamble will hang in there and do just that.

Where Have You Gone?

ARTIS GILMORE

The Gentle Giant

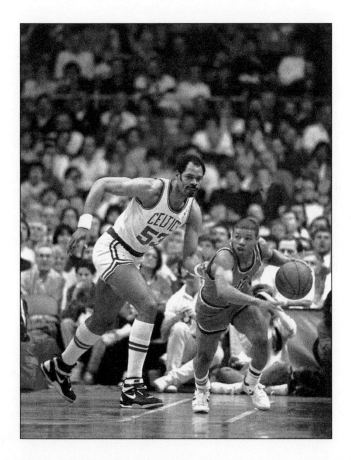

ARTIS GILMORE

**College: Jacksonville | Height: 7'2"
Weight: 265 lbs. | DOB: 09/21/1949 | Position: Center
Years with Celtics: 1987-'88**

Notes: Third-team high school All-American. Averaged 20 points and 20 rebounds per game in two years at Division I Jacksonville. Led the nation in rebounding as both a junior and a senior. As a senior, led Jacksonville to a 27-2 record and a matchup with perennial power UCLA in the NCAA Championship Game. Selected by the Chicago Bulls (NBA) and the Kentucky Colonels (ABA) in 1971. Honored as both the ABA Rookie of the Year and as the league's Most Valuable Player, finishing 10th in the league in scoring, first in rebounds, and first in field-goal percentage. Played five All-Star seasons in the ABA, producing staggering statistical numbers and leading the Colonels to the ABA Finals twice, both against Indiana. Won ABA Championship, 1975. Six-time NBA All-Star as a member of the Chicago Bulls and San Antonio Spurs. Played 670 consecutive games. Named to *Sporting News'* Top 50 of the first 50 Years of the NBA. Enshrined in the Naismith Memorial Basketball Hall of Fame.

He is no longer on the outside looking in, no longer the possessor of the unofficial title "Best Player Not Enshrined in the Naismith Memorial Basketball Hall of Fame." His résumé, bursting with 24,941 points, 16,330 rebounds, and 2,497 blocks spread over 17 professional seasons and two leagues has finally been recognized. Today Artis Gilmore—a former high school All-American who later helped lead Jacksonville to the NCAA Championship Game, an ABA superstar who posted 12 solid NBA seasons after that league folded, an 11-time All-Star with a streak of 640 consecutive games played—stands tall among the greatest basketball players to have ever played the game. He also stands out as one of its most humble.

Gilmore: "As a youngster growing up in Chipley, Florida, I admired those great basketball legends of the day, players like Bill Russell, Wilt Chamberlain, Jerry West, Oscar Robertson, and the like. They represented what makes this sport so significant on so many levels and in so many ways. Looking back at that era in basketball history, they were clearly recognized as some of the greatest basketball players this sport had ever produced. That sentiment hasn't changed in all of the years that have passed since their glory days in the 1960s. These players continue to be universally admired and respected. Their accomplishments shine today, and their imprint on the game continues to be felt by millions of fans who have never seen them play. I never imagined that one day I might share a stage with them as a member of the Naismith Memorial Basketball Hall of Fame."

Gilmore is also quick to give credit to his family for their unwavering support.

"Without the Lord Jesus Christ in my life, none of this would have been possible. My mother, my wife Enola Gay, my five beautiful children— each of them has played a significant part in my career and in my inclusion in one of the most exclusive clubs in the world. Without them none of this would have been possible. I am truly blessed with a loving, caring, and supportive family."

Now living in Jacksonville, Gilmore works for W.W. Gay Mechanical Contractor, Inc., in the area of private development. The company is based in Jacksonville, Florida, where he once led Jacksonville University to the NCAA title game against mighty UCLA.

"We do commercial estimating, HVAC, design/build, a whole host of things," he says. "I am currently focused on customer relations and private development, and I have played a part in turning W.W. Gay into the largest mechanical contractor in the southeast. It is very satisfying work."

Gilmore's long and illustrious basketball career may be behind him now, the rebounds and blocks replaced by Rolodexes and boardrooms, but it remains a frequent topic of conversation. Small wonder; when you are world famous for your exploits on the hardwood—and 7'2" tall to boot— the subject tends to come up from time-to-time.

"Every day," he says matter-of-factly. Whether opening doors of potential clients or simply thrilling those who remember his stellar play, Gilmore is approached wherever his goes. "People recognize me every day, and they want to talk about some aspect of my career."

And while the player affectionately known as the "A-Train" may have seen his last NBA stop as a member of the Boston Celtics, this during an abbreviated 47 game stint during the 1988-'89 season, Gilmore holds to Red Auerbach's credo of "Once a Celtic, always a Celtic."

"While my role was limited with the Celtics, I certainly enjoyed my time spent with the Celtic organization. For the first time in my NBA career I was able to play deeper into the playoffs than I had my previous 11 years. And it was truly a professional organization. Today, many of the other NBA organizations are similar in the way they treat the athlete, but that wasn't always the case. The level of professionalism wasn't the same, and the other franchises have had to play catch-up. Something as simple as uniforms is a prime example. The Celtics always made sure that the uniforms were clean and ready for the players, whereas this task was the player's responsibility everywhere else that I played. That has all changed now. All NBA franchises take care of the uniforms."

Much has changed for Gilmore since growing up poor in rural Chipley, Florida. Back then his family could barely make ends meet, and there were times when food was hard to come by. Jobs were scarce, race relations tense, and the future seemed as bleak as the craggy roads connecting this small town of 5,000. Still, his parents were convinced that young Artis could make something of himself. They instilled in him a strong value system, with a premium on things such as morals and character, and a belief that education was the key to a better life. Gilmore paid attention. He attended an all-black school—this was pre-integration—and he stayed out of trouble, sidestepping the dual temptations of drugs and alcohol while pursuing his first love, football. A growth spurt, coupled with a minor football injury, turned Gilmore's athletic focus to the hardwood. The family moved to nearby Dothan, Alabama, prior to his senior year of high school, and the 6'9½" responded by being named a third-team All-American. The sky seemed the limit, yet it took a two-year stop at Gardner-Webb Junior College in Boiling Springs, North Carolina for Gilmore to reach his full athletic potential.

"I ended up at Gardner-Webb simply because my grades were very poor," he says. "It was a two-year school at the time, but by the end of my second year it had become a four-year program. The coaches wanted the players to stay, but several of us decided to move on. I looked at Jacksonville, and decided that it was right for me."

Playing in Jacksonville meant being closer to home, and this was a huge plus for the gifted pivot man. Now 7'2" with the musculature of a young Wilt Chamberlain, Gilmore instantly transformed the Dolphins into a collegiate power, as the team went 27-2 during his senior season and reached the NCAA championship game. Awaiting them: legendary coach John Wooden and the mighty UCLA Bruins. Gilmore staked Jacksonville to an early lead, but Wooden was able to adjust his lineup and neutralize the Dolphins' advantage underneath the basket. It proved to be the difference in the game.

"We played well," Gilmore says, reflecting what could have been. "We were not intimidated, and we certainly didn't idolize UCLA. We were ready to compete, but I'm not so sure that we played our best basketball. Sydney Wicks had an extraordinary game against me. There was always a question of some of the shots that were blocked, and whether they were goal-tending, but Sydney was very aggressive in going to the basket. He deserves credit for playing so well."

Despite the loss, Gilmore did nothing to diminish his standing as the top center in collegiate basketball. He averaged 20 points and 20 rebounds during those two seasons in Jacksonville, and found himself coveted by both the NBA and the ABA. The Chicago Bulls drafted him, as did the Kentucky Colonels of the ABA, and Gilmore was faced with his first big decision as a professional.

"I had a very young attorney, and what I thought was a very good support group in Jacksonville. They advised me that [signing with the ABA] was a great opportunity to do some things right away for my mother and father, who were certainly very special people in my life. So I wanted to make sure that I could give something back to my parents. At the time, the ABA was the quickest way to do that."

Gilmore's transition to professional basketball was seamless. He led the Colonels to a 68-14 record that first year, earning the Rookie of the Year and the Most Valuable Player awards for his outstanding play. Statistically, he finished 10th in the league in scoring, first in rebounds, and first in field-goal percentage, but it was the intangibles that really made the difference. Gilmore was an intimidating presence underneath the basket, forcing opposing teams to alter their game plans—and opposing players to alter their shots.

"I was still in college when I started to believe I could succeed at the professional level," Gilmore says. "There was a gentleman named Bones McKinney—he worked with me, and told me that I could very easily make the transition from college to the pros."

McKinney, a former Boston Celtic, proved to be prophetic in his analysis of the young center. Gilmore played five seasons in the ABA, producing staggering statistical numbers and leading the Colonels to the ABA Finals twice, both against Indiana. By 1975, Gilmore and the Colonels were champions of the ABA.

"We had a very good coach in Hubie Brown," recalls Gilmore. "We had Dan Issel, Louie Dampier, Ted McClain, and Bird Averitt to name a few. It was a very competitive, very smart group of players, and we were able to play very well together."

The ABA would fold a year later. However, Gilmore remains very proud of his ABA roots.

"The three-point shot, the Slam Dunk Contest, those things were introduced in the ABA," he says, smiling. "The ABA was viewed as a more free-wheeling league, and as a league not caught up in the stodgy tradition of its NBA counterpart. The ABA was very willing to take chances— whether that meant going after the best players or trying to lure NBA referees over to the ABA. It was a great experience for me, and the ABA's imprint remains visible and relevant today."

With the ABA-NBA merger official, the Chicago Bulls would have the first overall pick in the dispersal draft. In a draft that included such talent as Moses Malone and Maurice Lucas, Chicago wasted little time in snatching up one of the best big men in basketball. A slow start that first season—the Bulls would open with 13 consecutive defeats—was more than offset by the strong finish, as Gilmore led Chicago to 20 wins in the final 24 games. During this stretch he erupted for 32 points, 17 rebounds, five assists, and four blocks against the Seattle Supersonics, and 29 points and 23 rebounds against the Philadelphia 76ers.

If there were any doubters about Gilmore's ability, he proved them wrong by posting numbers comparable to those put up while playing in the ABA. He averaged no less than 17.8 points during his six seasons with the Bulls, playing in all 82 games five times. His durability was as a professional was remarkable—Gilmore played in a mind-boggling 670 consecutive games, a number almost unheard of when it comes to the warriors who battle underneath the boards.

"Robert Parish was another iron man," Gilmore says, referring to his former Celtic teammate. "He was an extraordinary player, and I remember the transaction that sent him from Golden State to the Celtics. . . . he seemed to be a perfect fit. It turned his whole career around. It turned him into an extraordinary person as well as a great, great center. He had such a good understanding of the game. He understood his role, especially playing with players like Larry Bird, Kevin McHale, Nate Archibald, and Danny Ainge. To be compared to him in any way is very flattering."

While Gilmore was named an All-Star in four of his six seasons as a Bull, the team struggled to advance in the playoffs. He asked to be traded following the 1981-'82 season. The San Antonio Spurs were the recipient of this good fortune, as Gilmore gave that franchise five solid years in the paint. The first season, Gilmore and the Spurs reached the Western Conference Finals, where Kareem Abdul-Jabbar and Magic Johnson awaited.

"The Lakers were very talented, well-coached, and deep," he says. "We played them hard—I think I played Kareem as well as anyone in the league—but we just couldn't stop them."

After five seasons in San Antonio, the team was in a rebuilding mode. Gilmore was traded back to the Bulls, where he played 39 games during the 1987-'88 regular season. He then found himself traded again, this time to Boston.

Does Gilmore have a fond memory of his time spent as a Celtic?

"To this day, Larry Bird remains one of my closest friends. We talk by phone quite frequently. As members of the Boston Celtics, we had a chance to reflect on some of our earlier times together, like the time we spent together in Panama City. Larry was at Indiana State then. Even further back, when he was living in French Lick, Larry would come to the Kentucky Colonels games, so we had a chance to talk about that. So spending time with Larry was very special for me."

GERALD HENDERSON

The Steal That Saved a Championship

GERALD HENDERSON

College: Virginia Commonwealth | Height: 6'2"
Weight: 175 lb. | DOB: 1/16/1956 | Position: Guard
Years with Celtics: 1979-1984

Notes: Won two championships with Celtics and one as Detroit Piston. In 13-year NBA career, played for six teams. As a rookie, mentored by Hall of Fame point guard Nate "Tiny" Archibald. His steal against Lakers in '84 playoff final is one of the great moments in Celtics history.

There were 18 seconds on the scoreboard clock and the Los Angeles Lakers were ahead, 113-111, in Game Two of the '84 championship series. Kevin McHale had just missed two free throws and Lakers Coach Pat Riley decided to call timeout, which proved to be ill-advised. The Lakers, which had won the opener with a 115-109 win at the Boston Garden, were already celebrating because the Celtics, who were over the foul limit, would need a miracle to avoid heading to the Forum down 2-0.

As the Celtics positioned themselves defensively, LA forward James Worthy passed the ball in to Magic Johnson, who immediately fired the ball back to Worthy, who was standing ten feet in front of the Celtics bench. Spotting Byron Scott across the court near the three-point line, Worthy casually lobbed a pass towards his teammate. Sprinting in from midcourt, Celtics guard Gerald Henderson, anticipating the play, picked off the pass and raced to the basket for an uncontested layup which tied the score at 113-113.

"In my mind, I could hear Johnny Most screaming, 'Henderson stole the ball! Gerald Henderson stole the ball!' Fact was I had no idea the ball would be going to Scott," the Boston guard said afterward. "I was just running towards the nearest Laker to me, trying to put some defensive pressure on them."

But there were still 13 seconds to go, and LA had the opportunity to take the final shot.

With the ball in Magic Johnson's hands, the Lakers leader killed some time off the clock by dribbling back and forth 16 feet from the basket as Boston scrambled to get in position to contest a last-second shot. Magic, though, had lost track of time and failed to pull the trigger before the final buzzer sounded.

The Lakers were stunned that Johnson could have made such a mental error. Magic hung his head in disbelief. The tide had turned. Worthy, who had hit 11 of 12 shots from the field and finished with 29 points, was now the goat.

In the overtime period, Henderson again played a crucial role. With Boston ahead by a point, Larry Bird, being double-teamed, passed the ball to Henderson just above the key. As LA rotated to the ball, the Boston guard spotted forward Scott Wedman in the corner and, with two Lakers on top of him, managed to squeeze off a difficult pass. Wedman set his feet and buried the shot. Parish then stole the ball from Lakers center Bob McAdoo to seal the 124-121 win and tie the series.

"If Gerald hadn't made that steal," Bird said, "I think the Lakers would have eliminated us. Until that last 18 seconds of the game, everything was going their way."

"That pass I made still haunts me," says Worthy. "Worst mistake I ever made."

"People talk about my steal being one of the greatest moments in Celtics history, but the play I think was better was the pass to Wedman," says Henderson. "It was a split-second decision and the pass had to be perfect."

The MVP for the Celtics in their seven-game series win which earned them their 15th NBA title was Bird, who averaged 27.4 points and 14 rebounds. However, it was Henderson's steal which was replayed on TV and radio hundreds of times throughout and immediately following the series.

"I purposely didn't listen or watch the play for at least a month," says Henderson. "I had my own idea of how Johnny Most called the play, and I kept reliving the play and Johnny's call in my mind." When Henderson finally did hear Most's call, he was in for a letdown. Most didn't yell "Henderson stole the ball." Instead, the legendary play-by-play man put a different twist on Henderson's moment of glory.

"And it's picked off. It goes to Henderson and he lays it in. And it's all tied up. A great play by Henderson. They threw a crosscourt pass and Henderson anticipated it and picked it off."

"We were basically dead in the water until Gerald made that steal," said Boston center Robert Parish. "It really changed the whole complexion of the season, not just that game."

The championship, the second of Henderson's career, proved to his swan song with Boston. On October 16, 1984, he was sent packing in an ill-fated move by Boston for Seattle's 1986 first-round pick, which turned out to be the second overall choice, Len Bias, who passed away from a cocaine overdose two days after draft day.

Red Auerbach claimed the reason he traded the popular guard was because Henderson came to training camp out of shape. It was a ridiculous statement by the Celtics general manager. "Gerald didn't have an ounce of fat on him," said Cedric Maxwell. "Red always had to make the guy he was trading away into a villain. He had to justify every move he made. The sad thing is that the fans in Boston believed everything Red said. If he said the moon was purple, there were people who took his word for it."

The trade, in reality, made sense for the Celtics. Boston was overstocked with guards. Danny Ainge was becoming known as a deadly three-point shooter, Dennis Johnson, at age 30, was still one of the best defenders in the league, Nate "Tiny" Archibald was a premiere playmaker, 10-year veteran M. L. Carr was the team's most physical player and Rick Carlisle was a steady, tenacious rookie.

"I sort of saw it coming," says Henderson. "The younger guys needed to get more playing time, and I had some decent trade value, especially after we had just won a title. What bothered me were Red's remarks because they were unfair and untrue."

A graduate of Virginia Commonwealth, Henderson was originally a third-round draft pick of the San Antonio Spurs in 1978. Cut during training camp, he played for the Tucson Gunners of the Western Basketball Association where he led the team to a championship and won Playoff MVP honors. His speed and raw talent caught the eye of K. C. Jones, who convinced the Celtics to sign him as a free agent.

"There were four or five teams interested in me, but the Celtics offered me good money, all guaranteed," he said. "It was a young team, a rebuilding team, and they had a rookie named Larry Bird. I got a lot of experience my first year, playing about 15 minutes a game. The confidence I gained as a rookie really affected my entire career. It erased all doubts that I could play at the NBA level."

After the trade to Seattle, Henderson discovered not all teams were as close-knit as the Celtics. "There was a lot of in-fighting everywhere I went. With the Sonics, guys were concerned more about stats than wins. Then I was traded to the Knicks in 1986. Bernard King was injured the whole season and Patrick Ewing missed 18 games. Things were ugly because we had a different lineup almost every night. We ended up with just 24 wins. I was waived by the Knicks the next year and picked up by Philadelphia. By then, Charles Barkley was publicly stating that he wanted to be traded. He didn't think the owners were committed to winning. He played hard every night, but the team didn't have any depth. After two years, I moved on.

"In 1989, I was signed and then waived by Milwaukee. Ten days later, I was signed as a free agent by the Pistons. I thought I finally was back in a Celtic-like situation. I was 34 years old, and I knew I wasn't going to get much playing time. The important thing for me was that I was on a winning team. I hoped things would be somewhat similar to how the players had gotten along so well in Boston. But the times had changed. Guys did their jobs, but they weren't close. In Boston, we all hung out with one another. We'd all eat our meals together. We'd all kid around with each other, talking trash. Everyone looked forward to going to practice because we all loved to compete against each other. But, bottom line, during games we'd all root for each other to do well.

"In Detroit, everyone went to practice or a game and then went their separate ways. There was no camaraderie. We won the NBA championship, and I got my ring, but, as the song goes, the thrill was gone. I played 16 more games in the NBA, with Houston and then with Detroit in 1991-'92. Then I retired after a 13-year career. I've got no complaints. Not too many players win three championships and are lucky enough to play five years with the Celtics, the best team in basketball."

Today, Gerald and his wife, Marie, own an energy consulting firm in Philadelphia. They spend many of their weekends traveling around the league to watch their son, Gerald Jr., play for Michael Jordan's Charlotte Bobcats. "He's an entirely different player than I was. He jumps out of the gym. He's quicker, stronger and more aggressive. When he starts getting cocky, though, I just put on one my rings, wave it in front of his face and tell him I got two more hidden away. Then I ask him where his is. That keeps him humble."

CONNER HENRY

Dream Job

CONNER HENRY

College: California—Santa Barbara | Height: 6'7"
Weight: 195 lbs. | DOB: 07/21/1963 | Position: Guard
Years with Celtics: 1986-'87, 1987-'88

Notes: Starred at UC Santa Barbara, where he became the career leader in assists and scored 1,236 points, eighth all-time. Drafted by the Houston Rockets in the fourth round of the 1986 NBA Draft. Signed to the first of two consecutive ten-day contracts by the Boston Celtics on January 1, 1987. Made his Boston Garden debut six days later, going 4-of-5 from behind the arc. Re-signed for the remainder of the season on January 22, 1987. Waived on November 30, 1987.

Imagine doing something so well that you are granted membership into one of the world's most exclusive fraternities, where only one in every 10,000 is selected to perform before an audience of millions. Now imagine yourself sharing the stage with the preeminent talent in your chosen profession, at a time when history unfolds before you in unprecedented abundance, as if manna from heaven. You are there, in the middle of it all, plying your trade in the company of greatness.

Who wouldn't want to be you? Your stage is one of sport's holiest cathedrals. Your teammates are the reigning world champions, and you have joined them in their quest to repeat and build a dynasty. Your debut comes off as scripted in Hollywood, with shots falling from almost impossible distances and the throaty, hometown crowd roaring its approval. Future hall-of-fame players slap you on the back, wish you well and accept you as one of their own. And when that magical game is finally over, you walk away secure in the fact that you've made the most of a golden opportunity.

Your name is Conner Henry. And you, my friend, have arrived.

For legions of basketball junkies, simply making it onto the Boston Celtics roster is the dreamiest of dream jobs. It is a franchise steeped in history, a standard-bearer in the realm of championships, an icon so resplendent in its deal-closing that even now, nearly 20 years removed from its last title, the rest of the NBA can only look up at those 16 banners with a mixture of aspiration and envy. Now imagine being a Boston Celtic when the roster is populated with names such as Bird, McHale, Parish, and Walton. These men are the Mount Rushmore of low-post play, and here you are, feeding the ball to them in practice. In games they find you for spot-open threes, confident that you will bury the shot if given the opportunity. This would be enough for almost anyone, but there are more surprises to come; perhaps no defending champion in NBA history battled as much adversity as the 1986-'87 Boston Celtics, as a valiant playoff run would leave them two games short of their coveted repeat.

You and I can only dream of the perfect alchemy of place and circumstance. Henry lived it. He was there the night that Larry Bird stole the ball from Isiah Thomas, and he was there to witness that dagger of a baby hook by a man named Magic in the blast furnace otherwise known as the Boston Garden. Henry can tell you all about June basketball in the fabled Garden, about the heat and the rats and the obstructed view seating that gave the place its charm.

Conner Henry's journey from unabashed hoop addict to solid NBA player began in Claremont, California, where his father, Granville Henry, worked as a college professor at Claremont McKenna College. The elder Henry would go on to become recognized by the school as an Emeritus Professor.

"My father began teaching at the college as a math professor in 1959," says Henry, who served as an assistant basketball coach for the Stags for five years, starting with the 2001-'02 season. "I literally grew up at Claremont McKenna. Our house was directly behind the football field, which meant that you had to walk through the campus to get to it. I played on that field a lot as a child and have a lot of great memories of that part of my life. I was also involved in organized athletics very early on, serving as a ball boy in all three major sports at the age of five, so athletic competition came very naturally to me."

It was here that Henry gained unfettered access to the athletic facilities, gravitating to the basketball court in large part because of his lithe frame. He played for long hours, sometimes with others, sometimes alone, always dreaming of one day making it onto the game's biggest stage.

His idol was "Pistol" Pete Maravich, and Henry molded his game after the flashy guard, landing at UC Santa Barbara with a repertoire of fancy passes and a reputation for deadly long-range accuracy. He started right away, overcame an injured knee during his junior season, and finished atop the career assists mark in the school's record books.

"The injury was very frustrating," Henry points out. "It occurred during practice. I was in a full sprint when someone clipped my heel from behind and I fell hard on my left knee. I was lucky in one respect, because I only stretched the ligament and didn't actually tear it. The doctor equipped me with a steel knee brace so that I could continue to play basketball. The brace was considered top of the line back then, but by today's standards it was quite archaic. But it enabled me to continue playing, which, in my eyes, was the most important thing at the time. I didn't redshirt that season but, in retrospect, I probably should have taken the time to recover. I just didn't fully understand the dynamics of the injury. As it was, the team's starting point guard was also dragging that big, cumbersome brace up and down the court."

Brace or no brace, Henry excelled on the basketball court. As a senior, he displayed both poise and deadeye marksmanship in consistently leading UC Santa Barbara in a number of statistical categories. And although the Gauchos would never be confused with national power UCLA, Henry & Co. made things interesting for a number of ranked foes.

Says Henry: "We played the University of Houston when the team was ranked Number 1 in the country and also boasted Phi Slamma Jamma. They came to Santa Barbara with Hakeem [then known as Akeem] Olajuwon and Clyde Drexler, and everyone expected them to run us out of our own building. Our tallest player was 6'7", and he had to battle Olajuwon on the blocks. It was a great atmosphere. The Thunderdome was sold out, and they were still letting people in—the fire department must have turned its eye in another direction for this game. Houston jumped out to a huge lead, and was up by 19 points at halftime. We played incredibly well after intermission and nearly pulled off the upset, losing by two points."

The Houston Rockets drafted Henry in the fourth round of the 1986 NBA Draft—the same draft in which the Celtics would draft Maryland star

Len Bias. Henry played just 18 games in Texas before landing in Boston, where he quickly made a name for himself as a three-point specialist. Close friends with Dennis Johnson, Henry found himself on the Celtics' roster courtesy of the NBA's 10-day contract. Facing the Milwaukee Bucks in his inaugural home game with Team Green, Henry drained his first shot—a three-pointer—and energized the Boston Garden faithful with his hard-nosed play. He would finish the contest by converting four-of-five from behind the arc, finally exiting the court as the sellout crowd showered him with the spontaneous chant of "Ten more days."

Henry says, "It was a magical night. I had no idea something like that might happen, although we were playing the Milwaukee Bucks and I had a feeling that I'd get into the game. I was very excited, very nervous, but once I got into the game I was able to settle down. I got my legs underneath me, which also helped, but the main thing was being a member of the Boston Celtics. When you have players like Larry Bird, Robert Parish, and Kevin McHale to throw the ball to, you don't feel as much pressure to go in and make things happen. They command so much attention that good movement and ball rotation will put you in a position to succeed. And that's what happened. I got open and the first one went in. That relaxed me, and I was able to flow with the game the rest of the way. I kept moving and kept getting looks, and the shots kept going in. I'll never forget the chants from the fans. It was incredible. By the end of the game I was breathing extremely hard because I was somewhat out of shape. Everyone on the team made it a point to congratulate me, which certainly made me feel like part of the Boston Celtics."

Timing, as they say, is everything, and Henry's presence on the team coincided with some of the most memorable moments in Celtics history. Take Bird's steal from Isiah Thomas, for example. Regarded as one of the greatest plays in NBA history, Henry had a front-row seat for Larry Legend's game-saving—and, quite possibly, series-saving—theft. Only John Havlicek's legendary steal ranks higher in terms of late-game heroics by a Boston Celtic.

"From the sideline all we could do was hope for a foul or a steal," says Henry, "but with so little time left the likelihood of either happening was slim to none. A foul, maybe, but a steal? At the time you don't realize the true magnitude of something like that—you're overcome with excitement, but you just don't fully grasp the historical significance of that play. It's only later that you realize what you've been a part of. When I see the play today, I can look at it and know that I was involved. It's a great feeling."

That Celtics-Pistons series was also known for its intensity. Bill Laimbeer's takedown of Bird set the tone, as did Robert Parish's retaliation one game later. Who can forget the sight of Laimbeer, knocked to the floor, bloodied, while the Boston Garden faithful roared in approval?

"The NBA became a different place because of that series," Henry says. "Detroit's bruising style of play had never really existed at that level. The referees were letting them define their style, which was very physical and based on intimidation. The smothering defenses that you see today have their roots in what the Pistons were doing back then. Every possession was critical, and defending the basket became even more important than actually scoring on the offensive end."

Bird's steal kept Henry's dream season alive, catapulting him directly into the 1987 NBA Finals. The Lakers were the last hurdle left, but they were deep, talented and rested. The Celtics, by contrast, were worn out. Every series had been a battle. Players were hurt. The bench was thin. Still, much was hanging in the balance when Magic Johnson hit the infamous baby hook. That shot turned the series irrevocably in the Lakers' favor, and Henry's own magical run would soon be over.

Henry says, "Magic got the ball, turned, did that drive-whirl, and let go with the baby hook. Kevin and Robert played it perfectly, both of them extending as far as they could to defend the shot, but the ball went over both of them and into the basket. It was a terrible blow to us, and we felt it long after the game was over. Instead of squaring the series at two games apiece, we had to win that third game in the Boston Garden and then win two more in Los Angeles. Given the physical condition of our team, it was just too much to expect."

Looking back now, what memories of playing for the Celtics stand out the most?

"I was just an ordinary player on an extraordinary team," Henry says. "Bird, McHale, Parish . . . they were rock stars. You'd go from city to city and you'd get off the bus, and it was just an absolute rock star atmosphere. Fans everywhere—at the hotel, the restaurants, all the places that we went. It was crazy like that everywhere."

There's another memory that stands out after all of these years, one in which Henry was tasked with guarding arguably the greatest player in the history of the NBA.

"Michael Jordan," Henry says, smiling. "We were playing the Bulls, and this was during a time when Jordan was averaging close to 46 points-per-game over a month span. I guarded him for close to a quarter, and he maintained that scoring average. He had 12 points in the quarter on me, including an alley-oop dunk where he kicked me in the head."

Following retirement, Henry returned to Claremont McKenna and worked as the Associate Director of Career Counseling from October 2001, until September 2006. From there, his career path took an unexpected turn when college pal Scott Fisher coaxed him into an assistant coaching position with the Perth Wildcats of Australia's National Basketball League. Fisher was the head coach at the time.

"I love the game of basketball and Scott is a great friend. It was an exciting opportunity and a great way for me to stay involved in the game."

After a two-year apprenticeship that began in June 2006, Henry slipped into Fisher's shoes as the head coach of the Wildcats. It was a position he would hold for one season, and while Fisher eventually returned home to the United States, that didn't mean Henry was left Down Under without a support system.

"Scott listened to our games and followed them closely. He'd follow us nightly when we played, and I'd usually have an email from him the next morning."

Following his one-season stint as the Perth head coach, Henry decided to remain in Australia and accepted an assistant coaching position with the NBL Sydney Kings. He held this role for two seasons, and is currently head coach of the Northern Suburbs Bears of the Waratah Championship

League. Through it all, Henry's passion for the job is obvious. He's a vocal coach who rarely sits.

"Sometimes my emotions boil over and I do lose my mind on the sideline," Henry says, a twinkle in his eye. "But it's also fun. I love what I'm doing."

It's clear to see that Henry has found his calling in life. And while coaching basketball is his new dream job, the memories of the old one are still very much alive. He can close his eyes and see Robert Parish, hobbled by a severe ankle sprain, battling Bill Laimbeer and the Detroit Pistons on one leg. He can see Kevin McHale gutting out another superb performance on a broken foot. He can see Bird's steal and Magic's hook, and he can take satisfaction in knowing that he was there as hoop history was being written.

The rest of us should be so lucky.

BAILEY HOWELL

The Natural

BAILEY HOWELL

College: Mississippi State | Height: 6'7"
Weight: 220 lbs. | DOB: 01/20/1937 | Position: Forward
Years with Celtics: 1966-'67 through 1969-'70

Notes: All State (1954, 1955) and All-American (1955) player at Middleton (TN) High School. First Team All-America (1959) at Mississippi State. The *Sporting News* First Team All-America (1959). Second-Team All-America (1958). Three-time All Southeastern Conference (1957-'59). Southeastern Conference MVP (1958, 1959). Led the nation in field goal shooting (.568) in 1957. Enshrined in Mississippi and MSU Halls of Fame. Six-time All Star (1961-'64, 1966-'67) Member of two NBA championship teams with the Boston Celtics (1968, 1969). Enshrined in the Naismith Memorial Basketball Hall of Fame on September 29, 1997.

He spent his entire athletic career collecting awards—first garnering All-State and All-America honors in high school, then consensus All-America recognition in college, and finally All-Star status in the pros—so it is only fitting that Bailey Howell's name is now on a trophy of his own, a rugged likeness of himself awarded annually to Mississippi's top men's college basketball player. The Cellular South Howell Trophy made its debut on April 14, 2005, with Lawrence Roberts, a 6'9" senior center at Mississippi State University, being named the first recipient. For the modest Howell, the award served as a reminder of how far he had come in his life, from those long days in the cotton fields of the Deep South to the legendary parquet of the Boston Garden.

"I'm very grateful to be recognized in this way," says Howell, ever the gentleman. Retired and living in Starkville, Mississippi, the Hall of Fame legend was on hand for the first-ever presentation ceremony in Jackson. Since then, four other men have been honored with the Howell Trophy, most recently two-time recipient Jarvis Varnado. And while these men have all been humbled by their selection, it's the man with his name attached to the trophy who seems the most taken aback. "I honestly never dreamed that my name would be associated with something like this. It's a great honor."

"Bailey really is a very genuine person," says Michael Rubenstein, Executive Director of the Mississippi Sports Hall of Fame & Museum. "He is very humble, but he must have had some deep level of inner toughness to have averaged an unbelievable 20 rebounds a game as he did his senior year at Mississippi State. It's very appropriate that the award was named after him."

Cast in bronze and walnut and weighing over 40 pounds, it is also fitting that the inaugural Howell Trophy went to Roberts, who is known for his rebounding prowess. Howell thrived on the boards.

"Oh, I've seen his numbers," said Roberts, who was a second round selection by the Seattle Supersonics in the 2005 NBA Draft. Roberts played two seasons with the Memphis Grizzlies, and now plays for the Lithuanian pro club BC Lietuvos Rytas. "I've seen the records. They're way up there. Winning the award, and both me and him being great rebounders, that's another plus."

Hoops were almost effortless for this human rebounding machine. From the first time he picked up a basketball, Bailey Howell possessed a gift that very quickly set him apart from his peers. He was a natural on the court, at home within its geometric confines, a player so skilled that at the time of his retirement from the NBA in 1971, Howell ranked among the league's top 10 in nine statistical categories. But statistics only tell part of the story. Howell, who grew up near the cotton fields surrounding Middleton, Tennessee, never made himself bigger than the team. Regardless of his star power, he was always willing to subjugate his considerable game for the bigger cause. Such characteristics explain how Howell, a six-time NBA All-Star, blended perfectly with Bill Russell's Boston Celtics, winning two world championships as the curtain closed on arguably the greatest sports dynasty ever.

But it wasn't just natural ability that set Howell apart. It was the strong work ethic, instilled by his parents that helped to make him special on the basketball court. For Howell, his days were spent working the fields or helping with chores around the family homestead. It was a simpler life back then, with very little in the way of distraction.

"Middleton was a very small town of maybe 300 people or so," says Howell, "and our family actually lived plumb out of the city limits. It was a rural, farming community with no industry to speak about. Tennessee Gas built a pump station there during my teenage years, with lines running from Texas and Louisiana on up into Tennessee. Other than that, the area was mostly made up of farms and small businesses.

"Basketball was the only sport offered at our high school. There were no football or baseball teams for the students, so we'd play pick-up games whenever we could. Our school year started in early August because we would turn out in late September, during the cotton harvest season. Basketball practice didn't start until after we resumed our classes, but we would get together on our own and practice whenever we could.

"We played basketball most of the year. After the regular season was over we would play in the regional and class tournaments, and then we'd play informally through the spring and summer. We only attended school eight months out of the year—we were always out in May, so that we could help chop cotton—so it was important to have a sport to play when we weren't working."

Howell excelled on the hardwood, earning All-State honors in 1954 and 1955. As a senior he averaged 32.1 points-per-game.

"Following my senior season, I was selected to play in the annual Murray State High School North-South All-Star Basketball Game. I played well, grabbed a bunch of rebounds, and was selected to the All-American team. They don't play that game anymore, but back then it was one of the most prestigious events in high school basketball."

Following graduation, Howell enrolled at Mississippi State University. There were plenty of other offers, but the raw-boned forward wanted to play in the SEC. He had plenty of other choices—Kentucky came calling, as did Tennessee and the University of Mississippi—but MSU proved to be the best fit for the versatile power forward. Like Larry Bird at Indiana State decades later, Howell found himself more comfortable on a smaller campus with a more relaxed atmosphere. And it was at MSU that his virtuosity shone through; in an era when big men were planted firmly around the basket, Howell displayed a guard's shooting touch from the outside. He was a glimpse into the future of basketball, an offensive anomaly, and his presence on the court wreaked havoc on opposing defenses. Blessed with all of that talent, was Howell ever tempted to play for the legendary Adolph Rupp?

"James 'Babe' McCarthy was the Bulldog coach at the time, and he was a major reason that I decided to enroll at MSU. He was ahead of his time as far as recruiting was concerned—he visited me, and made a real effort to sell the school to my family. He made sure that other individuals from the basketball program visited as well. Kentucky showed some interest, but Rupp sent Harry Lancaster, his assistant coach, with a scholarship offer. That was it. MSU just did a much better job. It finally came down to MSU and the University of Tennessee, and Knoxville was just too far away from home."

As a three-year letter-winner, Howell led MSU to a 61-14 record over three seasons, and averaged 27 points-per-game. Back then, freshmen weren't eligible to play on the varsity team, so Howell's coming-out party didn't occur until a year later, when MSU defeated the highly-ranked Kentucky Wildcats. Howell torched Rupp's Kentucky Wildcats for 37 points, serving notice that he could excel against the best programs in the country. It was the first Bulldog victory over a UK team in thirty-five years. As a senior, Howell fulfilled another goal—winning the SEC Championship.

The two-time consensus All-America graduated from college on time, and with a treasure-trove of accomplishments to call his own. Among them: Becoming the first SEC player in history to reach the 2,000-point, 1,000-rebound club; producing a career-high 34 rebound performance against LSU (February 1, 1957); finishing as the leading scorer and rebounder in MSU history; leading the NCAA in field goal shooting as a sophomore (.568 in 1957); and capturing two Southeastern Conference MVP awards (1958, 1959).

For Howell, NBA basketball was the next logical progression. Urban legend has it that Cincinnati, choosing first, wanted to snatch the 6'7" rebounding machine to bolster its anemic frontcourt. But unable to reach contract terms prior to the draft, Royals management swung a deal with Detroit, allowing them to take Howell with the second overall selection. He was an All-Star by his second season, the first of six such honors.

The Pistons, however, struggled in the win column. During Howell's five years in Detroit, the team never finished better than second place in the standings. They were also unable to get past the Lakers and into the Finals. It was a frustrating period in Howell's professional life, but he never complained publicly. Nor did he demand a trade. Instead, he played five solid seasons for the Pistons, appearing in at least 75 games per campaign, while averaging more than 20 points and 10 rebounds over that span.

Struggling to improve, the Pistons traded Howell to the Baltimore Bullets prior to the 1964-'65 regular season. Howell's two seasons in a Baltimore uniform proved to be even more challenging than the previous five in Detroit. The Bullets struggled despite a talent-laden roster, and the lack of team harmony began to wear on the MSU product. All of that changed on September 1, 1966, when Red Auerbach sent backup center Mel Counts to Baltimore in exchange for Howell. It was a move that helped rejuvenate both Howell and the aging world champions; despite having their string of eight consecutive NBA titles snapped by the Philadelphia 76ers, the Celtics benefited immediately from Howell's offensive punch. His contributions factored heavily into the team's championship runs the following two seasons, giving Howell a pair of rings and the perfect capstone to a hall-of-fame career.

Says Howell on joining the Celtics: "It was a big thrill to go from a club with mediocre success to a team that had won eight NBA championships in a row. I got to play with players like Sam Jones, John Havlicek, and Bill Russell, which was very special for me because they were such special people. The Celtics were the defending champions when I arrived, but they were aging together as a team. The key players were brought in at roughly the same time, and the team always had the last pick in the draft. That made it much harder to bring young guys along, so Red offset this by making trades to improve the team. Willie Naulls is a good example of this. Don Nelson and Wayne Embry played for the Celtics because of Red's shrewdness.

"Mel Counts was a backup center, a seven-footer who couldn't shoot from outside. And because Russell was playing 48 minutes a game, Counts never got the opportunity to play. Red used this to his advantage. He had an unknown commodity, so he built Counts up in the eyes of the Baltimore brass. There was a glut of forwards on the team at the time, thanks to a trade with New York, and there wasn't really a center on the roster. Johnny Kerr was at the end of his career, and he was dealing with back problems. Bob Ferry wasn't really big enough to play center. So when the Bullets traded Walt Bellamy to the Knicks just eight games into the 1965-'66 season, the team began to explore trade opportunities. They decided to part with either a Bailey Howell or a Gus Johnson in order to get their center. It was a big break for me."

In 1967, the Celtics had their streak of eight consecutive NBA championships snapped. Many experts thought that Boston was too old to win another title, but in 1968 that's exactly what happened. For Howell, what was it like to finally win an NBA championship?

"It was very satisfying," he says in his familiar southern drawl. "We won that '68 title by beating the Lakers in six games, the last of which was in Los Angeles. That didn't surprise me, because our road record that year was outstanding. We took two of three road games against Detroit in the first round of the playoffs, three-of-four from Philly in the Eastern Division Finals, and then two-of-three from the Lakers to win it all. Philly had the best record in the league again, with basically the same club that won the title the year before, and we finished even farther behind them in the standings. But we played better at the most crucial times. We won Game 1, Game 5, and Game 7 in Philly. In our minds, it was the Sixers, with Chamberlain, that presented the biggest obstacle to winning it all. We were favored to beat the Lakers, and we dominated them.

"The next year Wilt was traded to Los Angeles. They weren't the same without him, and we beat the Sixers 4-1 in the opening round. New York was developing a really good club at that time, with players like Willis Reed, Walt Frazier, Dick Barnett, Dave DeBusschere, and Bill Bradley. They were the up-and-coming team, but we beat them head-to-head and ended up facing the Lakers again in the Finals.

"We barely made the playoffs that season. People often forget that fact. We were 48-34, but we were able to put it together in the playoffs. The Finals against the Lakers was a tough, competitive, hard, monumental struggle. We prevailed, but I remember having no energy left after it was over. I was so tired, but it still felt great because we'd won another championship."

Howell would play one more season, for Philadelphia. On September 29, 1997, he received basketball's highest honor—enshrinement in the Naismith Memorial Basketball Hall of Fame. Standing at the podium before a large contingent of family and friends, Howell thanked those closest to him as he reflected on a lifetime of hard work and dedication. He displayed the same humility that he'd carried with him since childhood, and then he walked away, a true southern gentleman, proud of his accomplishments but unwilling to make any bigger deal out of them. To those who know Bailey Howell best, his acceptance speech was as genuine as it was natural—a true reflection of the man himself.

"That hall of fame induction was icing on the cake for me," Howell says. "Many of my heroes—the people that I admired and looked up to— were already in the Hall of Fame, so it was a thrill to join them. I really don't have the words to describe what I felt that night. It was a great evening. I was very proud—most of my family was there, so it was one of the big highlights of my life. To be recognized in my profession as one of the people who achieved, as one who tried to reach my full potential . . . it was a very humbling experience. I'll never forget it."

On February 7, 2009, Howell was recognized again, this time by Mississippi State University. At halftime of the game between MSU and Arkansas, Howell became the first Bulldog basketball player to have his jersey retired. It was a packed-house event, and the standing ovation—and chants of "Bailey Howell!"—nearly left the honoree speechless.

"That was so special," he says, smiling fondly at the memory. "In fact, I think it's the highest honor that could ever be bestowed on anyone who has worn the maroon and white. And it's something that wouldn't have been possible without all of the people who've influenced and supported me along the way—my family, my coaches and my teammates, just to name a few. Mississippi State University is certainly a school that serves the citizens of Mississippi and the people throughout the world. I'm very proud to have been honored in this way."

Howell continues to stay close to his alma mater, remaining very active in MSU fund raising. He spends most of his time and energy working with the Bulldog Club, which helps to raise money for MSU athletic scholarships. He's also very active in his church, serving as an elder at the Starkville Church of Christ.

"My faith is very important to me," he says humbly. "I live to serve God, and I'm very thankful for the life that He has given me. Giving back is the least that I could do."

XAVIER McDANIEL

The X Factor

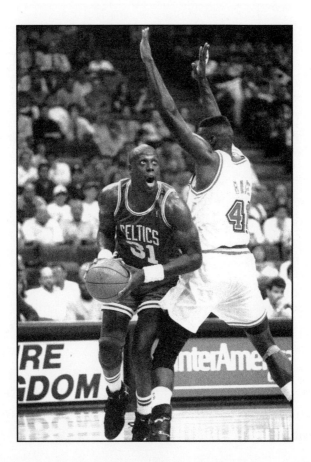

XAVIER McDANIEL

College: Wichita State | Height: 6'7"
Weight: 232 lbs. | DOB: 06/04/1963 | Position: Forward
Years with Celtics: 1992-'93 through 1994-'95

Notes: Led A. C. Flora High School (Columbia, South Carolina) to a state championship. Consensus All-America at Wichita State (1985). First player in NCAA history to lead the nation in both scoring and rebounding in the same season (1984). Led the nation in rebounding twice. Fourth overall selection, by the Seattle Supersonics, in the inaugural NBA Draft Lottery (1985). First-team All-Rookie with Seattle. Named Basketball Digest magazine's co-Rookie of the Year, along with New York's Patrick Ewing. Traded to the Phoenix Suns on December 7, 1990. Played one season with the Knicks ('91-'92). Signed by the Boston Celtics as a free agent on September 10, 1992.

The Seattle Supersonics had the fourth overall selection in the 1985 NBA Draft, and with it they hoped to lay the foundation for a championship contender. It was the first year of the draft lottery, and while Patrick Ewing was the obvious overall choice, going to the New York Knicks and taking a giant bite out of the Big Apple, everything else that followed was wide open. With Wayman Tisdale and Benoit Benjamin going to the Pacers and Clippers, respectively, the Sonics wasted little time snatching up the first player in collegiate history to lead the nation in scoring and rebounding in the same season.

That player was Xavier McDaniel, and over the next several seasons the player known as "X" and "X-Man" did indeed become a part of the Sonics' playoff foundation. Today, McDaniel is involved in laying foundations of his own. The owner of "34 X-Man, LLC," this one-time Boston Celtic buys undeveloped property in Columbia, South Carolina, subdivides it into lots, and then builds homes on them from the ground up.

"After basketball I pretty much chilled," McDaniel says, explaining his lifestyle in the weeks and months following retirement from the NBA. "My first few years I lived off what I made. Ask anyone that knows me, and they'll tell you that I take care of my money. Ask Robert Parish, and he'll roll his eyes and say 'McDaniel—that cheap bastard!'"

That frugality, combined with a keen business sense and a strong work ethic, has helped McDaniel turn his dream into reality—or, in this case, realty.

"I got started with a friend," he says of his venture. "We would buy existing homes, fix them up, and resell them. A few years later I branched out on my own. A few years ago I added a janitorial business to the mix. With the recent problems in the real estate market, building and selling homes became a lot tougher. It made sense to diversify."

The oldest of six children, McDaniel started playing basketball for the Ben Arnold's Boys Club in Columbia. He was a seventh grader at the time, and by the end of the season he was the league's MVP. Interestingly enough, hoops wasn't his first love.

"I played baseball and football from the age of eight," he says. "In the state of South Carolina, you either play one or the other. Basketball was just something to do in my spare time."

Only 5'10" in the eighth grade, McDaniel was years away from developing the intimidating persona that worked so well for him in the NBA. It is hard to imagine an adolescent X-Man, complete with Afro, but that was Xavier McDaniel circa 1976. He continued to play baseball and football, while finding time to indulge himself in the hobby that would later bring him fame and earn him millions.

"I grew from 5'10" to 6'7" in high school," he says of his development into cage intimidator. "I went through some hard times in high school, not doing my schoolwork, not doing the things necessary to be a student-athlete, and I thank God that I had a very good high school basketball coach. He could have been one of those coaches who did anything to keep his players eligible, but he told me that if I wanted to play on the team, I had to do my schoolwork. I played scrub minutes in the beginning, and I was a starter as a senior. I came back for my senior season mad, because I knew I should have been a starter, I knew I should have been on the All-Area team, because at 15 years old, I was already a star in Columbia, South Carolina. I didn't play my junior season, but that motivated me. I came back and had one of the best statistical seasons anyone in the state had ever put up."

Fueled by that anger, McDaniel led A. C. Flora High School to a state championship. He was the star on a team that produced four Division I college players, including Tyrone Corbin, who would go on to play for nine NBA teams in sixteen seasons. "X" averaged 18.8 points and 14.4 rebounds for the A. C. Flora juggernaut, while logging barely more than two quarters per game. His dream of playing at South Carolina seemed like a mere formality at that point, or at least until McDaniel opened the newspaper and was met with disappointment.

"I saw where the school had signed six guys," he says, "and they didn't have any more scholarships. They wanted me to go to prep school, so I decided to look elsewhere. I went to Clemson, Memphis State, and Wichita State on recruiting trips. I had a great time at Memphis State, so that made it hard as far as making my decision. I kept flip-flopping between Memphis and Wichita. I finally told myself I'd sleep on it and pick one the next morning. And I did. I woke up, and told my brother that I was going to Wichita State."

The decision proved to be a wise one. McDaniel had a stellar collegiate career, becoming the first player in NCAA history to lead the nation in both scoring and rebounding in the same season. Only two others have done so since. He also led the nation in rebounding twice, and in the process was named a consensus All-American. By the time his college career was over, McDaniel had elevated himself into an NBA lottery selection.

"I enjoyed my career at Wichita State. I know I made history with the scoring titles, but it never meant a lot because I never won the NCAA championship. At the time I was one of 46 players to score 2,000 points. I grabbed more that 1,300 rebounds—I don't know where I stand now, but at the time that put me second on the all-time list behind Wes Unseld. But I didn't win a championship. Individuals goals are okay, but team goals were always more important to me."

With the exception of the first choice, the '85 NBA Draft was rife with suspense. There was plenty of talent, but few can't-miss projections beyond Ewing. Karl Malone was taken with the 13th pick, behind such names as Jon Koncak, Joe Kleine, and Kenny Green. McDaniel arrived at Madison Square Garden wide-eyed and nervous, unsure as to when his name would be called. He watched as Ewing made his way to the podium to shake Commissioner Stern's hand, followed in short-order by Tisdale and Benjamin, and then he began to feel a tremendous sense of anxiety.

"We were sitting in a line," McDaniel says. "All four of us. Ewing went first, then Wayman and Benoit, and then I was just sitting there hoping that my name would be called. I didn't want to be sitting there by myself, waiting for a team to pick me. And when they called my name, I just thanked God that I was able to do something for my family. Anyone who knows me knows that I would come to the gym with jeans and sneakers on. I would have played the game for free. But to be able to take care of my family and still do something that I love . . . that's what made it so special."

Like his good friend Ewing, McDaniel was an instant success. He averaged 17.1 points and 8.0 rebounds as a starter during his first season. He was also named first-team All-Rookie and Basketball Digest co-Rookie of the Year (along with Malone).

"Patrick won the NBA Rookie of the Year award," he says, smiling. Casual acquaintances on draft day, Ewing and McDaniel have formed a close friendship through the years. The two men are now like brothers, and rib each other good-naturedly. "I tell him all the time, that he should give me my damn trophy back. Patrick will say, 'Man, but I put up numbers,' and I say, 'But you got hurt and only did it for 50 games. I did it for 82 games!' We joke a lot about that. I tell him I'm going to come over to his house and steal my trophy from him."

McDaniel, with his head shaved clean and that intimidating, trademark scowl on display during games, could hardly help contain the joy he felt when away from the court. And who could blame him? The man who grew up idolizing Dr. J was suddenly competing against him. The man who imagined himself as Wes Unseld, or Bobby "Greyhound" Dandridge, or Elvin Hayes was wearing an NBA uniform and playing at some of the same venues.

"I took a little bit of something from all of those guys," gushes McDaniel proudly. "Bobby Dandridge and the Big E—Elvin Hayes—had the turnaround jump shot, and that's the shot that I had to have. I told myself that I was going to master that shot. Dandridge used to shoot it for the Washington Bullets and Milwaukee Bucks. The Big E used to get down on those blocks and shoot it. Unstoppable. Wes Unseld and Moses Malone were all about the rebounding. Those were my guys. People don't give the outlet pass a lot of recognition, but Wes Unseld was the best ever at doing that. If you go back and look at the history of college basketball, he was right there at the top and I was probably second. I could throw the two-hand outlet, I could throw the one-hand baseball pass—and I could throw both of them right on the money. So these are some of the things that I tried to learn from the guys I watched and admired."

The Sonics improved during McDaniel's second season in the league, shocking the heavily favored Dallas Mavericks in the first round of the playoffs. He turned in a 29-point gem in the deciding game. The once-downtrodden Sonics were now building on the foundation of McDaniel, sharpshooter Dale Ellis, and the versatile Tom Chambers. All three players would average more than 20 points-per-game during the 1986-'87 season, a feat that they would duplicate a year later. Gradually, however, the rebuilding momentum stalled. Chambers was eventually moved, and Shawn Kemp was drafted in the first round of the 1989 NBA Draft.

McDaniel played 15 games for the Sonics during the 1990-'91 season, before being traded to Phoenix. The X-Man was less than a perfect fit for a Suns team that boasted Kevin Johnson, Chambers, Jeff Hornacek, and Dan Majerle, and the following season found himself paired with good pal Ewing in New York. With a formidable frontline of Ewing, McDaniel, and Charles Oakley, the Pat Riley-coached Knicks won 51 games before meeting Michael Jordan and the Chicago Bulls in the Eastern Conference Semifinals. The intense series went the distance, with Jordan & Co. prevailing in the seventh game.

"There ain't very many games that I said I couldn't get up and walk away from, but I was so sore after that one. It was so physical. It was a brutal war out there—the whole series was like that—but I felt like we should have won that series. We lost Game 1 in Chicago, but came back and took Game 2. Patrick had an unbelievable game. I just felt like we had championship potential, but we didn't get the job done when it counted. The Bulls won the series, and went on to win it all."

A contract dispute ended McDaniel's stay in New York after one season, and the unrestricted free agent was available to any team interested in his services. The Boston Celtics wasted little time making contact with X. As the talks progressed, he found out firsthand what is was like to negotiate with the legendary Red Auerbach.

McDaniel says, "When I came on my visit to Boston, Red laid the numbers out on the table. He said, 'We know you're worth more than this, but this is all we've got.' Then he said, 'Xavier, being a Celtic is more than money. And now that we've put this money on the table, you ain't leaving this room until you give us an answer.' So I asked him to leave the room for a minute, because I needed to make one phone call. I didn't want to call my girlfriend, I didn't want to call my momma. I told [agent] David Falk that I needed to call one person—Patrick Ewing.

"So Patrick answers and I say, 'Man, he's got me cornered. He's got me cornered in this room and he won't let me out without an answer.' I asked Patrick what to do, and he tells me to do what's right for me. Red comes back in, we talk some more, and after about 15 minutes I sign the contract. Red shakes my hand and says, 'Welcome to the Celtics family. When you become a Celtic, you become a Celtic for life. No matter where you go in this world, the door is always open as long as I'm alive.' That meant a lot to me."

X-Man played three seasons for the Celtics, this at a time when the franchise was going through significant transition and tragedy. Larry Bird retired prior to his arrival, Kevin McHale and Robert Parish were in serious decline, and Reggie Lewis died of a heart attack following the 1992-'93 season.

"Reggie was a very good person," McDaniel says, "the kind of person who was always helping people. Great leader. When Chris Ford took me out of the starting lineup, Reggie stood behind me and told coach that he needed to get X back in the lineup. I told Chris that I didn't mind coming off the bench, but Reggie and I worked well together. We had a play that we ran—if he went over the top I'd look for him, or if he went underneath he'd fade to the corner. It was all based on what the defense gave us. But we'd run that play and it was very successful.

"He was a community-minded guy who always got out and did things for those less fortunate than himself. I just sat in bed and cried when I heard that he'd died. It hurt a whole lot. It hurt so much that that's all I could do—just sit in my room and cry. I miss Reggie."

McDaniel finished his three-year contract with the Celtics, and found the team moving in another direction. He played two more seasons in the NBA, both with the New Jersey Nets, before retiring 20 games into the 1997-'98 campaign. After retiring, McDaniel appeared on Spike TV's televised SlamBall, where he coached the Riders squad in 2003. He has also made several appearances on the reality TV game show *Pros vs. Joes*.

And while X is never far from the spotlight, there is another member of the McDaniel family making noise on a national level. Heavily recruited Xylina McDaniel, a 6'2" forward from Spring Valley High School in Blythewood, South Carolina, will play her college ball at North Carolina.

"I've been very involved in my daughter's basketball career," McDaniel says. "It's been fun being a part of her AAU team, the South Carolina 76ers, and also being able to help guide her through the recruiting process. It really came down to three schools—Connecticut, South Carolina, and North Carolina. It was a difficult decision for her to make. She was having trouble deciding, so we met as a family and eliminated UConn. Narrowing it down to two schools really helped. She chose UNC, and she's really excited about her decision."

If she plays with the same intensity as her famous father, her future is very bright indeed.

Where Have You Gone?

GLENN McDONALD

Two Minutes of Glory

GLENN McDONALD

College: Long Beach State | Height: 6'6"
Weight: 198 lbs. | DOB: 03/18/1952 | Position: Forward
Years with Celtics: 1974-'75, 1975-'76

Notes: First-round draft choice (17th pick overall) by the Boston Celtics in 1974. Member of '76 championship club. Waived by Boston on October 21, 1976.

If not for his clutch shooting performance in the third overtime of what is almost universally regarded as the most exciting game in NBA history, Glenn McDonald might just be another obscure bench player whose name and stats appear among the hundreds listed on the Celtics' all-time roster. Instead, the reserve guard became a Boston legend in a matter of less than two minutes.

The heroics took place on June 4, 1976, in Game 5 of the Celtics Suns playoff finals, which was knotted at two games apiece. In a game that had numerous bizarre moments, Boston seemingly appeared to have won the game in the second overtime when John Havlicek nailed a jumper as time was expiring to give the Celtics a 111-110 advantage. However, as the fans celebrated by mobbing the court, referee Richie Powers ruled that there were still two seconds remaining because Suns guard Paul Westphal, the former Boston Celtic, had signaled for a timeout immediately after Havlicek's basket. Phoenix, though, had no timeouts left and was assessed a technical foul, which Celtic guard JoJo White converted.

Although now down by two points, Phoenix was able to put the ball into play from halfcourt, thanks to Westphal's quick thinking. On the ensuing play, Suns forward Garfield Heard took the inbounds pass from teammate Curtis Perry and fired in an 18-foot jumper to tie the score at 112-112 and force still another overtime.

Boston seemingly had lost its momentum. And when starting power forward Paul Silas became the fourth Celtics player to foul out with less than two minutes left in the third overtime, head coach Tommy Heinsohn had few options. He gambled by bringing in the 6'6" McDonald instead of the more experienced and taller Steve Kuberski.

"I wanted fresh legs out there," explains Heinsohn. "Both teams were exhausted. Glenn was the fastest guy I had. All I told him was, 'Mac, run 'em every chance you get.' Kuberski was a better rebounder than Glenn, but, in that situation, I wanted someone who could outrun the opposition."

Having hit only five of 23 shots up to that point in the playoffs, McDonald was surprised to get the opportunity to play at such a crucial stage of the game.

"As soon as Silas fouled out, I told Kuberski, 'You're going in. Take off your warm-ups,'" remembers McDonald. "But when Heinsohn motioned for me instead, I was ready. As a bench player, you prepare for a moment like that. You practice hard every day, hoping you'll be on the court in that type of situation. Plus, I wasn't totally cold. I had played seven or eight minutes in regulation, just coming in a few times to give guys a breather."

With 1:35 remaining in the third overtime, McDonald put in a layup to give the Celtics a 120-118 lead. On the next Celtics possession, a John Havlicek pass set up the guard for a smooth 10-foot fall-away jumper over Phoenix guard Dick Van Arsdale, padding Boston's lead to four.

Fittingly, it was McDonald who snared a defensive rebound, drew a foul, and confidently sank two free throws to clinch a nerve-wracking 128-126 victory for the Celts.

"The free throws went right through the net. I just stepped to the line with the attitude that I couldn't miss. Both of them went in pretty easy. After the game, it didn't really hit me that people would focus on my contributions as much as they did," McDonald says. "I knew I had played well, but we still were only up 3-2 in the series. It wasn't until later that night when I couldn't get any sleep that I realized how much of an impact my points had in that game. Suddenly it was like I was in awe of what had taken place."

After the Celtics earned their 13th championship by defeating the Suns, 4-2, McDonald fully realized precisely how much he had accomplished during Game 5 when he earned his two minutes of fame.

"I'd hear the replay of Johnny Most's calls on the radio, or I'd pick up a newspaper and see my picture on the front page of the sports section," he recalls. "Fans would come up to me and just start cheering. It was just an unbelievable time for me."

An All-American at Long Beach State, McDonald was selected by the Celtics in the first round of the 1974 draft. "Until my senior year, I was strictly a defensive type of player," he says. "Some scouts were comparing me to Don Chaney because I was tall for a guard, had long arms, and loved to pressure whomever I was guarding. When Lute Olson took over as head coach at Long Beach before my last year there, he told me to always shoot when I got open. He really gave me the confidence to be more aggressive on offense. I scored fairly well and started to get noticed by some scouts."

As the draft approached, McDonald thought the Bucks would take him with the 18th pick. "I knew they had seen me play a couple of times when I had played well," he says. "I had no idea that the Celtics [who were selecting one slot ahead of Milwaukee] had an interest. Obviously, I was absolutely elated that Boston knew about me and wanted me."

During his rookie season, McDonald played less than seven minutes a game, shooting 39 percent. He still has a clear recollection of his initiation into the league.

"One of my first games was against the Bucks in Milwaukee," he says. "Being young and being a rookie, I thought I had a nice running jump hook. Well, I made the mistake of trying to use that shot as I went into the lane. The ball barely left my hand when Kareem [Abdul-Jabbar] took one step towards me and slapped it over our bench and way up into the crowd. Every guy on the bench was howling with laughter. Even Heinsohn was doubled up. When something that embarrassing happens and you're on the court, there's nowhere to hide."

During the 1975-'76 regular season, the quiet reserve began to earn more minutes. "I used him quite a bit because he was one of those high energy guys that every coach likes to have come off the bench," recalls Heinsohn. "I liked bringing him in when we had a lead because he could force turnovers, block shots, and rebound well. I could use him to guard either a small forward or a big guard, whoever was a bigger scoring threat." So when McDonald finished the year by helping the Celtics win a title, he had every reason to be optimistic about his future. Ironically, though, the series against Phoenix would mark McDonald's final games with the club.

"I had gotten married in the offseason and was really looking forward to playing another season, maybe more, in Boston," he says. "But the team was making a lot of changes. Don Nelson was retiring, Silas was leaving to play for Denver, Sidney Wicks and Curtis Rowe were coming in. For whatever reasons, they made the decision to cut me in training camp."

The Bucks quickly signed McDonald as a temporary replacement for guard Fred Carter, who was out for a month with an injury. After playing just nine games, he was released. The next year McDonald was invited to the Suns training camp.

"The Suns had just drafted Walter Davis, so I knew the odds were against me," he says. "At that point, I decided I didn't want to go year to year not knowing where I'd be playing or even if I'd be playing. I didn't think it would be fair to my wife to always be uncertain of whether an NBA career would work out for us."

Opting to play overseas, McDonald signed a one-year guaranteed contract with Alvik in Stockholm, Sweden. That team won the Swedish championship and played in the European Cup competition. The adventure gave McDonald the opportunity to travel all over the European continent. It also gave him the motivation to snatch up a new job offer the following year. McDonald decided to spend one more season in pro ball in the Philippines.

"I discovered it was a very competitive league," McDonald recalls of his time in the Asian league. "My wife and I enjoyed living there, so we just kept going back-for eight more seasons."

In 1987, he retired and returned to his alma mater of Long Beach State where he became a part-time men's basketball assistant for two years. He moved on to become a full-time assistant coach for the women's team for two years and women's head coach for four seasons. Since 1996, he has been director of Intramurals at the college. He also works as an advance scout for the Utah Jazz.

In addition to his 18-year career at Long Beach State, McDonald was LA Sparks head coach Michael Cooper's top assistant when the team won back-to-back WNBA titles in 2001 and 2002.

"Working for the Sparks was another great time for me. To get a chance to be a part of a great pro team and a great staff was so rewarding," he says. "I'm just grateful my school was kind enough to have allowed me to take time off during the summers to accept the job."

Glenn and his wife, Renee, have been married 35 years and reside in the Long Beach area. The couple has two children: Michael, a former Stanford basketball player, and Alexi, a former University of Washington volleyball player.

"Every so often at one of [Long Beach State's] basketball games the scoreboard video screen will show a video clip of me during that Celtics Suns fifth game," he says. "Afterwards, a couple students will usually come up to me and say, 'Gee, Mr. McDonald, I didn't know you played for Boston.' Those comments really let me know how old I'm getting."

Where Have You Gone?

ROBERT PARISH

Hail to "The Chief"

ROBERT PARISH

College: Centenary | Height: 7'0"
Weight: 230 lbs. | DOB: 08/30/1953 | Position: Center
Years with Celtics: 1980-'81 through 1993-'94

Notes: Led Woodlawn (Louisiana) High School to state championship (1972), while being named All-American, All-State, All-District, and All-City. Named to the *Sporting News* All-America team while at Centenary College (1976). Led nation in rebounding twice ('74-'75 and '75-'76). First-round draft pick of the Golden State Warriors—the eighth overall selection in the 1976 NBA Draft. NBA Championships with the Boston Celtics (1981, 1984, 1986). Nine-time NBA All-Star (1981-'87, 1990-'91). Holds the NBA record for most seasons played all-time with 21. Holds the NBA record for most games played with 1,611. Retired with 23,334 points, then 13th best in history. Finished his career with 14,715 rebounds, then 6th best in history. NBA 50th Anniversary Team (1996). Inducted in the Naismith Memorial Basketball Hall of Fame on September 5, 2003.

His list of honors and accolades run almost as long and as deep as his 21 record-breaking seasons in the NBA, and yet Robert Parish remains as approachable as ever, stoic yet cordial, reserved yet gracious, a down-to-earth living legend with the soulful cool of a jazz musician. He is Louisiana born-and-bred, and yet his basketball legacy will be inextricably linked to the northeast, a delicious run that produced some of the biggest hoop moments this side of the Bill Russell Dynasty. Voted one of the NBA's 50 Greatest, Parish remained a certifiable star even into the twilight of his career, and the intervening years since his retirement have done nothing to dull the luster of his deeds. And on September 5, 2003, Parish produced perhaps his greatest slam dunk of all—induction into the Naismith Memorial Basketball Hall of Fame.

"One of the biggest nights of my life," Parish says quickly. "It was definitely the highlight of my career, because it's the ultimate compliment for anyone who is recognized in that way as a basketball player. Being inducted was a very proud moment for me, and it was also a very proud moment for my family. It was a memorable occasion, that's for sure. Something I'll never forget. We enjoyed all of the festivities. We enjoyed the whole weekend. It was a great experience."

Today, Parish enjoys life as a retired NBA legend, but that hardly means he sits still. He remains closely connected to the Boston Celtics, works as a basketball analyst for a Boston TV station, and serves as a basketball ambassador for the NBA.

"I travel and promote basketball for the NBA," Parish says. "I recently returned from Taipei, Taiwan, promoting basketball over there. I've been to New Delhi, India. It's something I really enjoy doing, because it takes me all over the world."

The globe-trotting Parish clearly loves his new gig, but after playing in a record 1,611 games over those 21 seasons, few could blame him for taking a little time off to recharge his batteries.

"I didn't do anything those first five years after retirement," he admits, laughing. "I just enjoyed the time off. Then I coached in the USBL for a year, with the Maryland Mustangs. I was involved with the NBA Legends Tour, which was a lot of fun, and I worked with Clifford Ray to run an annual big man basketball camp in Sarasota, Florida. I'm still involved with the Celtics as a consultant and mentor to the big men on the team, and I enjoy being a part of such a great organization."

And who better to teach big men than Parish? He is the NBA record-holder for seasons played (21) and games played (1,611) and is ranked second in playoff appearances (16) and fourth in total playoff games played (184). He also departed with four NBA World Championships, three as a member of the best frontcourt trio in basketball history. Mention Robert Parish and it isn't long before the names McHale and Bird are appended to the conversation. They are the Holy Trinity of front courts, the "Big Three," the engine behind those Celtic powerhouse teams of the 1980s.

Born on August 30, 1953, in Shreveport, Louisiana, Parish's parents were God-fearing people who provided as best they could for their son and insisted that he work hard in the classroom. Segregation and racism was very much alive and well at this time, yet Robert Sr. and Ada Parish did their best to insulate their four children from such ugliness. As a result, young Robert grew up confident and secure, although he was hardly enamored with the idea of playing basketball. He viewed it as work rather than fun, in part because he placed so much pressure on himself to excel.

By junior high school it was apparent to one person, at least, that he had the potential to do special things on the basketball court.

"If I had to pick one person who made the biggest impact on me in regards to basketball," Parish says, "it would have to be my junior high coach, Coleman Kidd. He stayed with me, kept encouraging me, and never let me give up on the game."

With Coleman refusing to let his protégée quit on himself, Parish entered the desegregated world of Woodlawn High School. It was a period of growth, both mentally and physically, and Parish found himself loving a game that he once considered drudgery. He flourished on the court, and seemed to grow taller with each passing day. Woodlawn reached the state finals two straight years with Parish dominating in the paint, garnering a state championship along the way. In 1972, he was named Player of the Year in the state of Louisiana. With nearly 400 scholarship offers to choose from, he decided to play collegiate basketball at tiny Centenary College—a mere six miles away from home.

"My parents were very instrumental in helping me to make a decision on where to go to school," he says. "Centenary College was a very good academic school, which was a big plus. It was also a small school, and that appealed to me for a number of reasons. From a basketball standpoint I preferred a smaller environment. I didn't want to go to a big program and be compared to all the great players who came before me, like a Lew Alcindor [Kareem Abdul-Jabbar] at UCLA, for example. Playing at Centenary allowed me to carve out my own identity and not get caught up in the comparison game.

"The coaches at Centenary were Larry Little and Rodney Wallace, and they put a lot of emphasis on schoolwork and education. Classes came first, and then basketball, not the other way around. This really impressed my parents. It was also very important to me, because I was the first one in my family to get a college education. And it was close to home."

While Parish continued his metamorphosis into one of the country's best centers, the Centenary basketball program was about to fall on hard times. As a small, independent school with no conference tie-ins, Centenary already faced a myriad of problems, such as recruiting players and scheduling games that didn't require extensive travel. Then, just days after Parish's signing, the NCAA punished the school for various rules violations. The probation would last for four years.

"The NCAA gave us a choice," says Parish. "We were informed of the sanctions, and told that we were free to transfer our eligibility to another college. There were a couple of factors that led me to stay. First, I had just become a father and I didn't want to move away from my child. That was very important to me. Secondly, it was a group decision by everyone eligible to transfer. There were six or seven of us. We met and talked about it, and as a group we decided to stay on at Centenary College."

A true student-athlete, Parish worked hard in the classroom and maintained an active social life on campus. He didn't own a car, choosing instead to walk wherever he needed to go. He stayed focused on the newest member of his family. He made his parents proud by receiving his degree in education. And amid all of this, Parish played extraordinary basketball.

It was a different era then, decades before 24-hour sports coverage, multimillion dollar endorsement contracts, and recruiting wars that reach down to the junior high level. Parish thrived in virtual obscurity, an unknown to everyone in the nation except those closest to the collegiate basketball scene. He averaged 21.6 points and 16.9 rebounds at Centenary, being named to the *Sporting News* All-America first team as a senior. He also led the nation in rebounding twice.

The Golden State Warriors wasted little time snapping up Parish with the eighth overall pick in the 1976 NBA Draft. Stoic and dignified, the rookie joined a veteran team that had won a championship in '75. His initial role was that of spectator. Rarely getting into games, Parish saw his minutes climb as the season progressed. His coach, Al Attles, kept encouraging Parish to practice hard and wait his turn, this even though the rookie never complained about his place in the rotation. He was unselfish to a fault.

His four years at Golden State were a mixture of promise and disappointment. The team was in decline, as players like Rick Barry were kept past their prime and young talent such as Jamaal Wilkes and Gus Williams were traded before reaching their full potential. Individually,

Parish continued to blossom. He became a starter, and he began to play like one of the premiere centers in the league. By his third season he was averaging 17.2 points and 12.1 rebounds per-game.

"It was a good time for me," Parish says of his four years in a Warrior uniform. "It was a learning experience, and I was fortunate to have a mentor in Clifford Ray. He took me under his wing and taught me all about being a professional athlete. He taught me about the professional work ethic, nutrition, and about taking care of myself both physically and mentally. That really made a big difference for me, because all I really had to do was concentrate on basketball."

By 1980 the Warriors were looking to rebuild yet again. The Boston Celtics possessed the top pick in the 1980 NBA Draft, two spots ahead of Golden State. Red Auerbach seemed set on drafting Purdue center Joe Barry Carroll, and yet he was hardly convinced that Carroll was the answer to Boston's own championship aspirations. So he shopped the pick. He offered to switch picks with the Warriors, on the condition that Parish was included as part of the trade. Golden State eagerly complied, touching off the single most lopsided trade in NBA history: While Carroll would go on to have a serviceable career with the Warriors, Rockets, Nets, Nuggets, and Suns, it was Auerbach and the Celtics who would reap three NBA championships because of the deal. Along with acquiring Parish, Auerbach would select Minnesota's Kevin McHale with the third overall pick—in Golden State's spot—giving Larry Bird superstar-caliber talent along the front line.

Just like that, the Big Three was born.

"The first day of Celtics training camp was very intense, very focused," Parish recalls. "It was almost like a playoff atmosphere. Every practice was like that. At first I didn't realize that myself, Larry and Kevin would become such a respected front line—we were all just trying to help the Celtics win a championship. And then, after Dave Cowens retired, it gave me a chance to see that we could be something special. I had fully intended to be Dave's backup. I had no idea that he would step away from the game so abruptly. So once Larry, Kevin, and I started playing together, I realized that we could be something special. Each of us had something to bring to the table—Larry could score from anywhere, and he was the best passing forward to ever play the game. Kevin had the long arms and the brilliant low-post moves. It all just came together."

With taskmaster Bill Fitch pushing his young charges, the Celtics steamrolled to a 62-20 record and a date with the Philadelphia 76ers in the 1981 Eastern Conference Finals. At stake: a chance to compete for an NBA championship. In an historic series, the Sixers, led by the nonpareil Julius Erving, forged a seemingly insurmountable 3-1 series lead. Yet the Celtics were able to fight their way back, winning three consecutive nail biters to advance. The poise of Boston's young frontcourt made the difference.

"I have to credit Coach Fitch for not giving up on us and for helping us to stay determined and focused. He instilled a mental toughness and a physical toughness in us. And even when we were down 3-1, he never let us doubt ourselves. He always preached that we could come back, that it wasn't over until Philadelphia won that fourth game, and that started from Day One in training camp. I believe that that's why we were able to prevail in that series."

The Celtics dispatched the Houston Rockets in the 1981 NBA Finals, winning the team's 14th championship. And while the NBA's most storied franchise was celebrating a rebirth, Parish's deeds that season were being admiringly serenaded by the Boston Garden faithful. Mistaken early on by television announcers as lustful boos, the chants were actually that of "Chief! Chief!"

"Cedric Maxwell nicknamed me 'Chief,' because when I came to the Celtics I was always talking about this movie, *One Flew Over the Cuckoo's Nest*. So Cedric finally saw it, and he said that I had similar characteristics of the Chief, because the Chief had them all fooled. He couldn't talk. He was a mute. And then it turns out that there wasn't anything wrong with the Chief. He was just hanging out there in that mental hospital, relaxing and taking it easy. Cedric said that I was stoic like the Chief."

While the Celtics came up short in the two seasons following that championship win over Houston, a four-game sweep at the hands of the Milwaukee Bucks in the 1983 NBA Playoffs was clearly the low point. Auerbach responded with two shrewd moves: He named K. C. Jones as the team's head coach, and he traded for defensive stopper Dennis Johnson.

"DJ fortified our defensive presence on the court," says Parish, "and he gave us a great point guard to replace the retired Tiny Archibald. People don't realize just how talented Dennis Johnson was, because he started his career as an off guard and finished it as a point guard. That's a huge transition, and he did it comfortably.

"I rank K. C. as one of the best coaches to have ever coached in the NBA. He was a great X and O coach, but he was also a great people person as well. He was great at relating to his players. One thing I admired about K. C. was that he was always able to make that eighth, ninth, 10th, 11th, and 12th guy feel like his opinion was just as important as one of the starters. I feel that's one of the reasons we were so successful under K. C. He was like Phil Jackson and Chuck Daly in that respect."

The Celtics responded, winning the 1984 NBA Championship in thrilling fashion. It was Celtics versus Lakers, East Coast meets West Coast, Bird against Magic. No Finals before or since has lived up to the hype.

"I was matched up against Kareem," he says, "and Kareem is the best player I've ever had to play against, period. No one was ever able to devise a defense to stop Kareem. He exploited every defense that was ever thrown at him. He was smart. He was intelligent. He was an extremely gifted athlete, and the only player I'd ever played against that I could never change his shot. That hook shot was automatic. He shot it the same way every time. Wilt Chamberlain was the only person who ever forced him to alter it. Fortunately, I was able to play him well enough to help us win that series."

The Celtics won it all again in 1986, with the addition of Bill Walton making this team arguably the greatest in NBA history.

"The 1986 Boston Celtics should be ranked as one of the best teams of all time," Parish says. "Easily in the top five, in my opinion. Bill brought toughness to the team, and a knowledge of what it takes to win an NBA championship. He was a part of that championship team with the Portland Trail Blazers, a former MVP, the best passing big man to ever play the game, and he brought great humility to the second unit. He was willing to put his ego aside for the good of the team. How many athletes of his stature are willing to take a lesser role in order to make the team better?

I had always respected Bill, and admired him from afar, because of the way he played the game on both ends of the court. That's how I prided myself. I worked on being consistent and multifaceted, and not just a one-dimensional player. That's the way that Bill Walton played the game."

The Celtics began a slow descent following that championship season, touched off by the tragic death of Len Bias just two days after the 1986 NBA Draft. The Big Three were forced to play major minutes, and this began to take its toll. By the early nineties, Bird, McHale, and Parish were shells of their former All-Star selves. Bird would retire first, followed closely by McHale, but Parish would hold up better than any other player in NBA history. He would play briefly for the Charlotte Hornets and Chicago Bulls, before retiring following the 1996-'97 season. After 21 seasons of stellar play, and a place as one of the NBA's "50 Greatest" of all time, Parish remains a Boston Celtic at heart.

"I will always treasure my time in Boston," he says. "All of the hard work, the championships, everything. And I'll never forget people like the late Johnny Most. He was chain smoker, and I remember Danny Ainge replacing his cigarettes with those exploding party poppers. Johnny would light one up, it would go off in his face, and then he'd grab another one. He went through four or five before he realized what Danny had done, and then he went on a swearing rampage. It was so funny. I can't remember ever laughing that hard."

As Parish travels to promote the league, he certainly has much to smile about. Few players in any sport have accomplished as much as the player known affectionately as Chief. He is a legend, but he remains the same dignified person who grew up humbly in Shreveport, honoring his parents while striving to make his mark in the world of professional basketball.

Where Have You Gone?

CHARLIE SCOTT

Family Man

CHARLIE SCOTT

**College: North Carolina | Height: 6'6"
Weight: 175 lbs. | DOB: 12/15/1948 | Position: Guard
Years with Celtics: 1975-'76 through 1977-'78**

Notes: The first black scholarship athlete at the University of North Carolina. Two-time All-America selection. Played in two NCAA Final Fours. Member of the 1968 gold medal-winning men's Olympic basketball team. Selected by the Virginia Squires of the ABA and the Boston Celtics of the NBA (1970). Co-ABA Rookie of the Year following the 1970-'71 season. Two-time ABA All-Star, his only two seasons in the league. Led ABA in scoring during the 1971-'72 season (33.4 PPG). Played three All-Star seasons for the Phoenix Suns. Traded by Phoenix to Boston for Paul Westphal and future draft choices on May 23, 1975. Member of the 1976 NBA World Champion Boston Celtics. Played in the NBA's "Greatest Game Ever," Game 5 of the 1976 NBA Finals between the Celtics and Suns.

Charlie Scott still looks the part. Whether making appearances on behalf of his current employer, Russell Athletics, or simply making the rounds in his hometown of Atlanta, Scott still looks as if he could take to the court and hang with today's NBA hotshots. Articulate, personable, and equally gracious, he is a throwback only in the sense of how he carries himself in the public eye. You won't find his name on the police blotter, and you won't find him writing tell-all books, à la Jose Canseco. Scott is whistle-clean, a devoted family man, and unabashedly loyal to the legendary programs for which he played.

"I bleed Tar Heel blue," he says, without hesitation, "and I'll always be a Celtic at heart. You won't catch me complaining about my basketball career, because things worked out pretty well for me, so I feel very fortunate to have had my career evolve the way it did. To be able to play college ball at North Carolina, and then end up winning a championship with the Boston Celtics, it just doesn't get much better than that."

Twenty-five years removed from his last NBA game, Scott has settled in Atlanta, where he lives with his wife and three children. He spends his free time watching his sons play basketball—Shaun, the oldest, is a member of the University of North Carolina JV team; Shannon, a McDonald's All-America, is a freshman at Ohio State.

"I'm very proud of them both," Scott says. "They're both enjoying the college experience in their own ways, and they're working hard to make their mark. As a dad, it would make me as proud as I could be if Shaun could make the varsity team, and the same if Shannon could make his mark on the Buckeye program. I love them both very much, and they know that I'm there for them every step of the way."

Scott also finds time to keep in touch with old friends like former Celtic teammate Jo Jo White, with whom he has a close connection. He enjoys reminiscing about his playing days in the old Boston Garden, calling it one of the greatest basketball arenas ever.

"The Garden was old and run down, the parquet floor had dead spots, and it was a sauna in June," he says, "but those things all worked to our advantage. The crowd was great—the most knowledgeable fans in basketball came to the Garden. I loved playing there."

These days Scott also enjoys working out to stay lean and trim. A little older, perhaps, his closely-cropped hair sprinkled with gray, but Scott looks as lean and trim as he did in his playing days.

"I eat at Subway," says Scott, laughing, when pressed for his secret to looking so good.

Scott's basketball roots can be traced back to Laurinburg, North Carolina, where he attended Laurinburg Academy High School. Described as "an itty-bitty town in the middle of nowhere," there is little else to do in Laurinburg but play basketball. The school has a rich basketball tradition; Chris Washburn, Sam Jones, and Jimmy Walker (Jalen Rose's dad) all played there, and Scott is quick to point out that jazz legend Dizzy Gillespie played the trumpet at Laurinburg before dropping out in 1935. Having made so many memories in the South—first as a high school standout and later as a two-time All-America selection at North Carolina—moving his family to Georgia made perfect sense.

"I lived in California from 1980 until 1990," Scott says. "Then I accepted a position with Champion, the athletic apparel company, and moved back to Atlanta. California was nice, but this is home.

"I worked for Champion for seven years as a sports marketing director, and then took a consulting position with Russell Athletics. My job is important to me. I enjoy my work. But I'm also focused on my family because, in today's society, a father has to be more involved with their kids. So between providing guidance and enjoying their extracurricular activities, I've taken a bigger role in their lives. I stay busy, but spending time with my family is very important to me. I really enjoy being involved with my wife and kids."

Born on December 15, 1948, in Harlem, Scott rarely missed an opportunity to participate in pickup games. He began playing organized basketball at the age of 12. He played bitty-ball first, then AAU ball, and somewhere along the line he fell in love with the game. By age 14 it was apparent that Scott was equally bright in the classroom. He attended New York's prestigious Stuyvesant High School, which specializes in mathematics, science, and technology. Some of the most renowned professionals in the country have attended Stuyvesant, and Scott hardly felt out of place.

But there was a downside.

"They didn't allow me to play on the basketball team," he says. "It was a high standards school, which helped me to prepare academically for life as a collegiate student-athlete. Stuyvesant also helped me to become more responsible."

He transferred to Laurinburg prior to his 10th grade season, and basketball was suddenly back on the radar. Three years later, Scott found himself being recruited by former Maryland coach Lefty Driesell, then the head coach at Davidson College. Practically signed, sealed, and delivered, Scott never really thought about playing anywhere else. He got along well with Driesell. He liked the campus. And at the time, Davidson was one of the premier basketball programs in the country.

"My mind was made up," Scott says, "Davidson was the place for me. But my high school coach talked me into looking at all of my options. He used to take me to watch the Tar Heels play. Deep in his heart, I think he wanted me to go to the University of North Carolina, so he was very persistent in making sure that I kept an open mind. And the more I visited the campus, the more I became enthralled with the school.

"As exciting as North Carolina was, it was equally hard to break the news to Lefty. He was the first person who really recognized me, noticed me, and gave me notoriety. I had gone to his basketball camp as a junior in high school, and that's when he offered me a scholarship. He told the world about me—no one had really heard about Charlie Scott before I attended Lefty's camp, but that all changed afterward. It was the start of a tremendous recruiting circumstance."

Scott's decision to play for the Tar Heels was groundbreaking. He became the first African American scholarship athlete in the school's history, helping to pave the way for other Carolina greats such as Phil Ford and Michael Jordan.

"It was a different time and place," says Scott. "Back then, African Americans didn't have a lot of players that they could identify with and cheer for. I was the first in many respects, and it was an honor to represent them the way that I did."

Represent them he did. In addition to being honored twice as an All American, Scott was All-ACC three times while leading the Tar Heels to two consecutive ACC championships and Final Four berths in 1968 and 1969. Ironically, Scott and Driesell would cross paths once more, this during 1969 East Regional final. With a trip to the Final Four at stake, Scott connected on 10 of 14 field-goal attempts in the second half, including a 20-footer with three seconds left to eliminate Davidson from the tournament.

"That was a big thrill," he says. "Scoring 40 points against Duke in the ACC tournament was really special. Those are moments I'll never forget. But the biggest thrill I ever had—and I think the biggest thrill that anybody has in that program—is simply being a part of North Carolina basketball. The camaraderie that comes by being there, by being a part of the team, by being part of starting the tradition . . . I think it's bigger than any one game or one moment. Ask anyone who has played there—Walter Davis, Michael Jordan, James Worthy—and they'll say that their biggest thrill about North Carolina was going to North Carolina."

Ironically, Scott was widely considered the best player in the ACC during his junior year, but the media didn't vote him the conference Player of the Year.

"I was extremely hurt," Scott says. "Losing the vote wasn't as stinging as the wide margin of the vote. But the important thing for me was to be the bigger person and not be bitter about it. I accepted it and moved on with the self knowledge that I had played well enough to receive stronger consideration than I received."

Thankfully for Scott, the snub didn't extend to the U.S. Olympic selection committee. Scott was invited to join the 1968 United States Olympic Team, where he would team with White en route to winning the gold medal. He was only 18 at the time.

"We were the last team to win the gold medal in consecutive order without any losses. It's a thrill and honor that becomes bigger as the years go on, just as it is to have played for the Tar Heels and the Celtics. I had the best of all worlds when it comes to basketball. I don't think I can be a person who moans and groans about my tradition of basketball and who I played for, and who I played with, and what we accomplished."

Following graduation, Scott was selected by the Virginia Squires of the ABA and the Boston Celtics of the NBA. He chose the former, setting into motion a series of events that ultimately lead him to the Boston Garden. He played two seasons for the Squires, being named Co-Rookie of the Year following the 1970-'71 season and being honored as an ABA All-Star both years. Although he teamed with a young Julius Erving during the 1971-'72 season, Scott yearned for the NBA stage. He bolted to the Phoenix Suns prior to the start of the 1972-'73 regular season.

Scott's time in Phoenix proved to be a mixed bag; he was an All-Star in three of his four seasons with the team, but the Suns were never serious contenders for an NBA championship.

"It was a great experience," Scott says. "Being in the NBA was everything that I thought it would be. I enjoyed playing in Phoenix, but we didn't have the type of personnel capable of playing against the Jerry Wests, the Wilt Chamberlains, the Willis Reeds, the Walt Fraziers, the Dave DeBusscheres. We just didn't have the personnel to win consistently against some very strong teams. Management was trying its best to improve the situation, but we were only wining 40-plus games a season and only two teams in each division were making the playoffs. So it was a humbling experience. I wanted to make the playoffs, I wanted to succeed at a high level, but we just weren't able to put it together and do the things that I was hoping that we could do."

All of that changed on May 23, 1975, when Boston traded the promising Paul Westphal and two picks to Phoenix for Charlie Scott. The Celtics had won an NBA crown in 1974, and the Scott-Westphal trade put the team on the fast track for yet another title. Suddenly, Boston could boast a backcourt of Charlie Scott and Jo Jo White, easily the best guard combination in the league at that time. Add players like Dave Cowens, John Havlicek, and Paul Silas to the mix, and the Celtics were positively lethal.

"I've always been a Celtics fan," says Scott. "I've always been in love with winning, so I knew that Boston was going to be the perfect fit for me. Red Auerbach was a living legend, a genius, and being able to play with guys like Cowens and Havlicek just made it that much more special."

The team won 54 games that season, before methodically working its way to the 1976 NBA Finals. Ironically, Westphal and the Suns awaited.

"It's funny how that worked out," Scott says, "but we were very confident about our chances of winning the series."

The Celtics would prevail in six games, garnering the team's 13th championship banner. The series is best known for that triple-overtime classic in Game 5, but Scott was dominant in the Game 6 clincher in Phoenix, with 25 points, 11 rebounds, five steals, and three assists. Scott smiles at the memory.

"I'm going to tell you what I told the media," he says proudly. "We never worried about Phoenix beating us in that series. People forget that we were up by 25 points in that triple-overtime game, and the Suns were somehow able to come back and force it into overtime. My hat goes off to them for that—it's called the 'Greatest Game Ever,'" and I'm glad to be a part of that, and it's great for folklore, but the honest truth is that we were never worried about losing that series. We had beaten them all year long. We looked at it player-to-player, and we couldn't see where we could be beat. Jo Jo White versus Paul Westphal—Jo Jo's going to win that. Me against Ricky Sobers—I'm going to win that. Paul Silas and Garfield Heard—Paul's going to win that. John Havlicek and whoever they're going to put out there on the other end of the court—doesn't matter because John's going to win that. Same with Cowens. So we knew we were going to win that series. There was no question about that."

The 1976 season marked the highlight of Scott's NBA career. He would play four more seasons, including a brief stint with the Los Angeles Lakers, before retiring as a Denver Nugget. Still, he considers Boston his NBA home.

"We shared a lot of things together as a team," Scott says. "I just enjoyed my whole time there. The friendships mean more than anything— to this day I remain close to Jo Jo. We get together as often as possible, and talk on the phone all the time. And that just goes back to the Tar Heels and the Celtics being like family. Once you play for these organizations you become a part of the family, and that's the way it will always be."

Where Have You Gone?

DEREK STRONG

Built for Speed

DEREK STRONG

**College: Xavier University | Height: 6'8"
Weight: 225 lbs. | DOB: 2/9/1968 | Position: Forward
Years with Celtics: 1994-1995**

Notes: Second round draft choice of Philadelphia 76ers in 1990. Played one season in Spain. Was MVP of Continental Basketball League in 1992-'93 before being signed by Milwaukee. Acquired by Celtics from the Bucks, along with Blue Edwards, for Ed Pinckney and Andrei Fetisov in 1994. In 10-year NBA career, played for six teams. Best season was with Orlando in '97-'98 when he averaged 12.7 points.

Growing up in Compton, California, Derek Strong's sports ambition was to become a stock car driver. His uncle built go-carts for some of the neighborhood youngsters and he lined up trash cans and rubber tires to form a track where the youngsters, mostly seven- and eight-year-olds, could race against each other.

However, the Strong family didn't have enough money to pay for Derek to join an official competitive league with a smooth asphalt track, so Strong decided to opt for basketball. His outstanding play in high school earned him a scholarship to Xavier University, where his aggressive rebounding and tenacious defense impressed the Philadelphia 76ers, who drafted him as the 47th overall, pick in the second round of the 1990 draft.

Because the Sixers refused to offer any guarantees, the 6'8" power forward headed to Spain to play for Huesca La Magia in the second division.

His first crack at the NBA came when Washington signed Strong to a 10-day contract in March of '92. He played in just one game, scoring three points in 12 minutes before the Bullets decided to release him. The following season he signed with the Quad City Thunder of the CBA, earning league MVP honors as well as being named Newcomer of the Year.

Signed by Milwaukee in February of 1993, he played in 23 games, averaging 6.8 points and 5.1 rebounds. As a reserve with the Bucks, Strong was frustrated. Playing almost exclusively at small forward, he shot only 41 percent from the field and simply did not fit in to Coach Mike Dunleavey's offensive plans.

His big break came in June of 1994 when Milwaukee traded him, along with Blue Edwards, to the Celtics for Ed Pickney and Andrei Fetisov. In Boston, he blossomed into an excellent rebounder and low-post scoring threat, shooting 45 percent from the field and 82 percent from the line. "We always viewed him as a power forward. Milwaukee had him playing 15 feet away from the basket. We wanted to take advantage of his strength. What we liked most about him was his defense," says then-Boston coach M. L. Carr. "He was 230 and all muscle. Once he established position, nobody could get inside of him to grab a rebound. We used him at all three frontcourt positions and he did a great job for us. He started getting a lot of respect around the league as someone who could score inside and never gave an inch when guarding All-Star type players. We wanted to re-sign him, but he was asking for more money and more years than we were willing to give."

After moving on to the Lakers on a one-year deal, Strong signed as a free agent with the Orlando Magic. Consistently playing 20 minutes a game, he averaged career highs in both scoring and rebounding. "Even though he was undersized, we played him at center quite a bit," said Magic head coach Brian Hill, "because he did well against guys like Alonzo Mourning, P. J. Brown, and even Shaquille O'Neal."

In his second year with the Magic, Strong had his best season as a pro, averaging 12.7 points and 7.4 rebounds. Nagging injuries, however, would plague Strong for the remainder of his career. After his fifth year in Orlando, he was traded to the Clippers, along with Keyon Dooling and Corey Maggette, for a 2006 first-round draft pick. Following one mediocre season, he was waived. He spent a year with the Columbus Riverdragons of the NBDL, he retired. "I had some injury problems and things just weren't working out. Even if I had gotten healthy, I don't think I'd have come back."

Still, he had a successful a 10-year NBA career, which few scouts originally thought would be possible.

With basketball behind him and money in his pockets, Strong decided to pursue his first love, car racing. In 2001, he became a professional stock car driver and formed a company, Derek Strong Racing, based out of Orlando, which was the first team to have two black female minority owners, Dawn Whitaker and Erica Hill.

"I started racing on tracks in Florida. In my first year, I placed fifth and eighth in two racetrack series," Strong says. "I keep trying to move up in the ranks. Right now I'm competing in the K and N Pro Series and some of the ARCA [American Racing Club of America] events. My goal is eventually race in the Busch League. Hopefully, if I can get to that level, my next step would be the Nextel Cup. We've had a few declines, but now we're finding the chemistry and I think we'll do well."

Strong, whose cars are custom fitted to accommodate his 6'8" frame, donates a percentage of his winnings to children's hospitals and to organizations that help youths. "I began to get involved in charity after I visited a children's hospital," the 44-year-old driver says. "It really touched me to see kids hooked up to IVs all day, confined to their units, and not knowing if they would live to see the next day. It was heartbreaking. They're just starting out in life, and they've been in the hospital every day fighting cancer and other illnesses. These kids should be on playgrounds, not in hospitals. If I can help them by donating money from my racing winnings, it just makes what I'm trying to accomplish just that much more rewarding."

Where Have You Gone?

RICK WEITZMAN

Looking after "Old Yella"

RICK WEITZMAN

College: Northeastern | Height: 6'2"
Weight: 175 lbs. | DOB: 04/30/1946 | Position: Guard
Years with Celtics: 1967-'68

Notes: A three-year letterman at Northeastern. Tenth-round draft pick (110th overall) of Celtics in 1967. Member of 1968 Celtics championship team.

There's nothing wrong with being a daydream believer. Just ask former Celtic Rick Weitzman. As a senior at Northeastern University in 1967, the 6'2" Brookline, Massachusetts, native had planned on pursuing a business career after graduating. While the former Husky starting guard admits there were moments during basketball practice when he would bury a jumper and fantasize about one day making that same shot after receiving a pass from Celtics All-Star guard Sam Jones, he realized such mental visualizations were nothing more than pipe dreams.

"In my three years on the varsity I averaged 12 points a game as an undersized shooting guard. I led the team in scoring my junior year, but I knew scouts weren't going to flock to see a guy on a team that played schools like Colby, Clark, Worcester Poly, Farleigh Dickinson, Boston University, the University of Rhode Island, and the University of New Hampshire," Weitzman says. "I had a lot of great moments at Northeastern. Now I was ready to move on to the business world."

Luckily, Red Auerbach saw enough of Weitzman to think he was worth drafting in the tenth round. The Celtics general manager happened to be in the Garden stands one night when Weitzman scored 24 points against BU late in the college season. He also was in attendance when the 21-year-old undersized shooter scored 28 points in a New England all-star game which was held a month before the draft.

Back in the '60s and '70s, it was a Celtic tradition to select local players late in the draft to generate positive publicity and also to fill out

Boston's rookie camp roster. The odds of Weitzman even surviving a week or two were astronomical.

"The Celtics had drafted seven guys ahead of me, including their top pick, Mal Graham, a guard who had a great career at NYU," Weitzman recalls. "They also brought in a couple of free agents. I thought for sure I'd get cut. Luckily, I probably played the best basketball of my life and was invited back to vets camp. I was ecstatic. Now, I had to prove myself against much stronger competition. I mean I was trying to earn a roster spot on a team that had won NBA championships in eight of the last nine years.

"The first day of camp was something I'll never forget. There I was out on the court with guys like Wayne Embry, Bailey Howell, Don Nelson, Satch Sanders, Sam Jones, John Havlicek, Larry Siegfried, and, of course, [player-coach] Bill Russell. I had grown up idolizing these guys and listening to my neighbor, Johnny Most, rave about their talent, guts and toughness during every one of his broadcasts. Needless to say, I was a nervous wreck as the practice began. Once we started scrimmaging, though, I relaxed and just played as hard as I could. For some reason I still can't fully explain, I played even better at veterans camp than I did in rookie camp."

Still, on the day before the regular-season opener, the Celtics had one more cut to make. After practice, Russell decided to have a two-on-two game among the four remaining rookies—Mal Graham, Johnny Jones, Neville Shed, and Weitzman. "All the veterans stayed to watch. It was the most physical, competitive, emotionally draining two-on-two contest I've ever seen," Weitzman says. "I was banging people around because if I was going to get cut, I wasn't going down without a fight."

The half-hour scrimmage ended when Shed hurt his knee. "Afterward, Russell didn't tell me I had made the team," says Weitzman. "I thought I had made the team, but no one officially said I had. So, the next night I just walked into the locker room, spotted an empty locker with a uniform hanging up, and started getting changed."

Weitzman's rookie season brought a lifetime of memories. "I was 21 years old, a teammate of so many All-Stars who had won five, six, seven championship rings," he says. "For me, it was mind-boggling to be on the best team in NBA history."

Throughout the year, the eager-to-please guard was assigned certain off-the-court tasks by the vets. "You know, sort of a hazing-type thing," he says. "For instance, when we were on the road, I had to carry a small, old, ugly yellow gym bag around. 'Old Yella,' as it was called, contained Bill Russell's crumpled, sometimes smelly, uniform. It was my responsibility to air out the uniform and then hang it up so it wouldn't look all wrinkled or stink too much when Russell wore it for the next game.

"One time, I forgot all about 'Old Yella' and Russell's stinky uniform. When he put the uniform on, you could see the steam coming out of his ears. Looking right at me, he yelled, 'Guess who's not getting off the bench tonight?'"

Then there was the time Weitzman was driving into the Garden during a snowstorm and there was a huge accident on the Mystic Bridge. "I was sitting in my car, thinking of how much I was going to get fined for being late to a game when I spotted John Havlicek jogging right past me," he recalls. "I yelled out, 'What are you doing? We're two miles from the Garden.' He told me to pull my car into the emergency lane and just leave it. The two of us then ran all the way to the Garden and actually made it to the game on time because it started late due to the weather. The only guy who didn't make it to the game, which we won, was our coach, Bill Russell. Red Auerbach had to coach the entire game. Russell finally showed up 10 minutes after the game ended. All Auerbach said to him was that Coach Russell had better fine his best player for missing the game. And make damn sure it's a steep one.'"

Weitzman played only 25 games in his first and only season as a Celtic. "But we won a championship, I got a ring, and I even scored four points in the championship game, including the final basket.

"There's tens of thousands of kids who would give anything to have the experiences I enjoyed that one year."

During the 1968 exhibition season, Weitzman injured his knee and was released. He returned to Northeastern to complete his degree and also played part-time for New Haven in the Eastern League, which was coached by former Celtic Gene Conley. After graduating, Weitzman taught English at Peabody High for 13 years. He also coached Peabody's basketball team for 10 years, compiling a 135-67 record.

"I was really proud of the kids I coached," he says. "Considering I took over a team which had zero wins the previous year, we proved that we could compete with anybody."

In 1980, Most recommended to his radio station general manager that he hire Weitzman to be the color commentator for all the Celtics broadcasts. "I wanted the job badly because Johnny was one guy who encouraged me to pursue basketball from the time I was just a little kid. To work with him, one of the game's legends, was another lucky break," he says. "Fortunately I was able to continue teaching while also broadcasting, because the officials at Peabody were very supportive and understanding. It was hectic and sometimes exhausting, but I loved it."

Weitzman's favorite broadcasting moment came one night when Boston was playing the Bullets in Landover, Maryland. "I asked Jeff Ruland, whom Johnny had nicknamed 'McFilthy,' if he would do a five minute pregame interview with us. Ruland asked if we were 'the guys from Boston.' When I told him we were, he screamed at me, 'My mom listens to you guys when you do our games and she says you're horseshit.'

"Well, I went back to Johnny and told him about Ruland's remarks, which really fired him up. Johnny was totally livid. He began the broadcast by delivering a message to McFilthy's mother: 'Mrs. Ruland, if you're listening, you'd better turn off your radio, because you're not going to like what you hear.' I didn't say too much during the game because Johnny went on a tirade against Ruland during each and every stoppage in play."

In 1982, Weitzman gave up his broadcasting job to become a volunteer assistant coach at his alma mater. At the same time, he accepted a part-time scouting position with the Celtics. By 1984, he was a full-time scout of college and CBA players for Boston.

Hard work and long hours paid off for Weitzman when Celtics General Manager Jan Yolk promoted him to head scout in 1987. "I set up rookie camp, chose many of the prospects we brought in, and arranged individual workouts for potential draft choices," he says. "I guess I'm most proud of two players I really believed in. The first, of course, was Reggie Lewis. While Reggie wasn't a huge secret around the league, he probably wasn't regarded as a first-round pick because Northeastern wasn't a big time program and he didn't play that well at the Portsmouth Invitational or in the Pizza Hut Classic. But because I had seen him play so often in college, I knew he had all the tools to be an excellent NBA player. The other player I really fought for in our pre-draft meetings was Rick Fox, who had a poor NCAA tournament for UNC. His stock really dropped because of that tournament. Twenty-three teams passed on him before we took him."

In 1997, when Rick Pitino came into power, Weitzman was fired. "I suspected I'd lose my job. New bosses always bring in their own guys," he says. "What bothered me was that Pitino didn't have the courtesy to tell me face to face that I was being let go. Instead, I received a phone call from Rich Pond, Pitino's right-hand man, telling me I was dismissed. Pitino didn't even have the class to call me himself. I had done a lot of draft preparation work. I figured, at the very least, he might want to pick my brain about my thoughts on the draft. . . . But I guess he figured he knew all the answers."

Once his days with the Celtics ended, Weitzman was quickly hired by the Cavaliers as a scout. "I knew Rick was a great evaluator of talent and a tireless worker. Honestly, I was surprised when Boston didn't keep him," says the former Cleveland GM Wayne Embry. "It wasn't just my opinion. Rick had a great reputation around the league."

When Embry was ousted from his Cavs position and Weitzman again found himself unemployed, Marty Blake, head of the NBA's scouting department, immediately contacted him and offered him a part-time job. In addition, ESPN hired him to handle color commentary for its international game of the week.

Then, seven years ago, Bernie Bickerstaff, who was about to be named GM of the expansion Charlotte Bobcats, asked Weitzman if he would be interested in a position with the new team. Weitzman jumped at the opportunity. "I was assigned to scout colleges and the NBDL. I was also involved in evaluating players at the postseason tournaments and at our pre-draft individual workouts," he says. "It was a great organization.

In fact, it reminded me of how the Celtics ran things when I was there, because there were good people there who know how to work together."

After working for the Bobcats for four years, Weitzman decided it was time to spend more time with his family and resigned his position.

Today, Weitzman is semi-retired. As a hobby, he conducts tours for fans at Fenway Park. "The Sox are a terrific organization. It's a fun job. It's great interacting with fans of all ages, especially the young kids. People really are curious about the history of Fenway and love to hear stories about the Red Sox, from Babe Ruth to Carl Yastrzemski to Kurt Schilling. I've learned a lot about the ballpark's tradition and what a tremendous place it is to watch a game."

Weitzman and his wife, Carol, reside in the Boston area and have two children, Alyssa and Jennifer.

Where Have You Gone?

BILL SHARMAN

Hall of Famer Times Two

BILL SHARMAN

College: Southern California | Height: 6'1"
Weight: 190 lbs. | DOB: 05/25/1926 | Position: Guard
Years with Celtics 1951-'52 through 1960-'61

Notes: Traded, along with Bob Brannum, by the Fort Wayne Pistons to the Celtics for the rights to Charlie Share in 1951. His No. 21 Celtics jersey was retired on October 15, 1966. Member of four championships teams while with Boston. Enshrined in the Naismith Memorial Hall of fame as a player and a coach.

His home office is a mini-museum, with hundreds of rare pictures, trophies, glassed-encased basketballs of historical significance, championship ring displays, jerseys, bats, and plaques lining bookshelves and covering almost every inch of wall space. Near his desk stands a lifesized cardboard photo image of the 86-year-old as a crew-cut young player wearing a No. 11 Southern California basketball uniform.

As Bill Sharman discusses his 60-year career in pro basketball, he uses the words "fortunate" and "lucky" to describe his remarkable success in the game he loves. Truth is, "luck" had nothing to do with it. The former Celtics guard, who was elected to the Hall of Fame for his achievements as a player in 1976, is a winner and a champion because of hard work, tremendous talent, intelligence, and, most importantly, an enthusiasm that only grows stronger with each passing year.

"I've been blessed," Sharman says. "I've been a part of 15 pro basketball championship teams—four as a player with the Boston Celtics, three as a coach, two as general manager of the Los Angeles Lakers, three as president of the Lakers, and three as special consultant for the Lakers. However, the one I remember and cherish the most is the Celtics' first championship in 1957 versus the St. Louis Hawks. We won [the seventh game] in double-overtime by two points. My shots weren't falling and Bob Cousy was struggling a little, but we had such a great bunch of guys that everyone just knew we'd find a way to win. . . . We had the ultimate confidence in one another.

"My whole experience in Boston was unbelievable. It was such a privilege and thrill to play for the great Red Auerbach. My teammates were the best, and the fans were always so supportive. I couldn't have asked for a better situation."

Regarded as the NBA's premiere pure shooter throughout the 1950s, the 6'1" Sharman led the league in free-throw percentage seven times, including five in a row. His reliable outside jumpers, usually set up by one of Cousy's on-target, often miraculous passes, were the perfect complement to the Celtics' inside attack, led by Bill Russell's offensive rebounding and Tommy Heinsohn's hook shots and 10-foot pull-up jumpers.

"Cousy would kid me about all the shots I got," recalls Sharman, who spent his first five Celtic offseasons as an outfielder in the Brooklyn Dodgers organization. "The funniest moment I had as a Celtic came in the '57 All-Star game at Boston. I grabbed a defensive rebound and spotted Bob all alone upcourt. I threw a full-court baseball pass towards him. He jumped for the ball, but it went over his outstretched hand and into the basket. As Cousy came back down the court, he faked being angry and said, 'Just like I always tell people, you never pass the ball to your teammate—even if they're wide open.'"

According to Auerbach, Sharman was more than merely a student of the game. "He was way ahead of his time," the former Celtics coach said. "On the day of every game, Bill would get up early in the morning and find a gym where he could work on his shot and his conditioning. Eventually I decided that if a great shooter like Sharman believed in it, then a light morning workout might help everyone on the team. That's how 'shootarounds' began. After we began doing it, every team copied us. Then there were also Bill's ideas about nutrition and proper rest. He ate specific meals at specific times. He knew the value of getting a good night's sleep. Every game day he took a nap for an hour. If he didn't get enough rest, he'd be angry with the world."

Sharman, who was selected to the All-NBA team seven times, helped the Celtics win four titles before retiring at age 35. "The guy probably could have played another three or four years, but I knew Bill was itching to coach," said Auerbach. "Whenever he was on the bench, he'd ask me a million questions about strategy, about substitutions. Almost every time he'd make a suggestion, it would be a good one. And I was smart enough to realize he had an incredible mind for the game."

That knowledge paid off handsomely for Sharman and the teams he coached. In his first year on the bench, Sharman's Cleveland Pipers won the ABL title. In 1971 he led the Utah Stars to an ABA championship. When he took over as coach of the Lakers in 1971, critics said his players were too old and too stubborn to be very "coachable." In particular, the media contended that Lakers star Wilt Chamberlain, at 35, would likely prove to be a major headache. At a casual preseason one-on-one meeting, Sharman managed to convince his 7-foot-1 center that fastbreak basketball and morning shootarounds would be the keys to success.

"If this team was going to win, I knew that Wilt and I had to get off to a good start. When I mentioned that I was going to have mandatory game-day morning shootarounds," Sharman recalls, "I expected Wilt, who had a reputation for being a night owl, might be upset at having to get up so often early in the morning. But, to my surprise, he didn't put up a stink. Instead Wilt told me, 'I'll go along with the idea, and we'll try it. If I think it will help the team, I'll do it.' Getting Wilt on my side from the beginning meant more than I can explain. He just had to buy into my beliefs, or the team would be in trouble."

LA proceeded to win 69 games that season as Chamberlain, bloodshot eyes and all, went through morning shootarounds without voicing a single complaint. With the team scoring more than 120 points a game for the season, Sharman's Lakers easily won the NBA title.

In all, the former Celtic guard coached 11 seasons before he was forced to leave the sidelines for good due to a mysterious vocal cord ailment which left his voice at a hoarse whisper. Six times he took his team to league finals, three times winning a championship. Along the way, he was voted Coach of the Year in the ABL (1962), Coach of the Year in the ABA (1970), and NBA Coach of the Year (1972).

"Not only was the man a tireless worker, he was an innovator. Bill was the first coach to study film on a daily basis," said former Celtics teammate K. C. Jones, who was hired by Sharman in 1971 to be the first assistant coach in Lakers history. "He did everything possible to make sure his team would be prepared, both mentally and physically. Because he regularly put in 18-hour workdays, his players believed and respected him. I mean totally.

"As a former player, Bill realized the importance of making sure everyone had a little fun at practices. For example, he might tell Wilt to play the point guard position in a scrimmage. Then everyone would break up laughing as Chamberlain dribbled upcourt and launched the funniest looking 25-foot jumpers you'd ever see. He found ways of livening things up rather than having the same old routine."

After leaving the coaching ranks, Sharman became LA's general manager. Directing the Lakers' personnel moves, he was instrumental is molding the '80 and '82 title teams. Choosing to leave the GM post in 1983 due to continuing vocal problems, Sharman became a special consultant to the Lakers, a position he still holds today. It is far from an honorary title. He regularly attends Lakers home games and then writes evaluation reports for both the front office and the coaching staff. When the team is on the road, he spends time scouting college talent on TV and with videotape.

Sharman's latest project is working as an executive producer on a documentary about the '71-'72 Lakers and their NBA record two-month winning streak of 33 games in his first year as Laker coach. "We had a powerhouse of a team," Sharman says. "We had Wilt, Jim McMillian, Jerry West, Happy Hairston, and Gail Goodrich in the starting lineup. It didn't take a coaching genius to pile up victories with those types of players."

Inducted to the Hall of Fame as a player in 1976, Sharman was reenshrined last year for his achievements as a coach. He joined John Wooden and Lenny Wilkens as the only men to be honored twice by the institution. Still an active golfer with a handicap of "ugh," as he puts it, Bill and his wife, Joyce, reside in Playa del Rey, California. They have four children and six grandchildren.

Where Have You Gone?

RICK ROBEY

The Bruiser

RICK ROBEY

College: Kentucky | Height: 6'10" | Weight: 235 lbs.
DOB: 01/30/1956 | Position: Center/Power forward
Years with Celtics: 1978-'79 through 1982-'83

Notes: Traded by the Indiana Pacers to Boston for Billy Knight on January 16, 1979. Member of the 1981 Celtics championship team. Traded to the Phoenix Suns for Dennis Johnson on June 27, 1983.

His name is the answer to one of the most frequently asked Celtics trivia questions: Whom did Boston General Manager Red Auerbach give up in order to obtain perennial All-Defense guard Dennis Johnson from the Phoenix Suns?

While Rick Robey would be remembered as the trade bait the Celtics used to snatch Johnson away from Phoenix in 1983, the 6'11" center-power forward was hardly regarded around the NBA as "chopped liver." In fact, at the time of the trade for DJ, Robey had enjoyed considerable success throughout both his college and pro careers.

As a starter for the University of Kentucky, Robey's inside presence helped lead the Wildcats to the 1978 NCAA championship. In the 94-88 title game victory over Duke, the 235-pound All-America dominated play in the lane by hitting eight of 11 shots, scoring 20 points and grabbing 20 rebounds. "We had a great bunch of guys," he says. "Our two main scorers, [small forward] Jack Givens and [shooting guard] Kyle Macy were pro material, both first-round picks. When they did miss an occasional shot, [center] Mike Phillips and I were underneath the basket to get the rebound and go up for the offensive basket. From the starters right down to the last man on the bench, we had perfect chemistry, very similar to the Celtic teams I played on."

Chosen third overall in the 1978 draft by the Pacers behind University of Minnesota big man Mychal Thompson, who was taken by Portland, and University of North Carolina point guard Phil Ford, Robey, as the backup to veteran center James Edwards, received limited playing during his first three months as a pro. "I was a little frustrated with how I was being used," Robey says. "But then, right after a Celtics-Pacers game, [Boston's player-coach] Dave Cowens walked up to me as we were walking off the court and tipped me off that Red Auerbach was trying to trade for me. I could have hugged Dave when he clued me in because I had always dreamed of playing for Boston."

On January 16, 1979, the Celtics did indeed acquire the rookie, sending veteran swingman Billy Knight to Indiana in the transaction. Robey's initial season in Boston was a learning experience for both the ex-UK big man and the team itself.

"Personally, I got schooled every day at practice because I had to go up against Cowens, who was an absolute madman," says Robey. "Dave was something else, man. He always played aggressively and physically, even against his own teammates. I didn't get a second to rest at either end of the court. He loved contact; so did I. He taught me a lot of little tricks that first year. I had more bumps and bruises from matching up against Dave in scrimmages than I got playing in the actual games.

"But the team was really struggling when I got to Boston. Outside of Nate Archibald, Cedric Maxwell, Jeff Judkins, and me, everyone we had was nothing but a journeyman. Plus, there were a ton of roster changes throughout the season. Dave was doing the best he could do as the coach, but things were just too crazy. One month he'd worry about how to handle [power forward] Marvin Barnes and the next month he'd be trying to figure out how to get some consistent production from Curtis Rowe, Sidney Wicks, and Bob McAdoo. I knew from the start that Red was going to clean house in the offseason. In the final weeks of the season, everyone knew Dave wanted to go back to being a full-time player and give up his coaching role."

Despite the fact that Boston ended up with a pathetic 29-53 record and finished dead last in the Atlantic Division, Robey was confident the team could reverse its fortunes practically overnight. The reason for his optimism boiled down to two words: Larry Bird, who, though drafted sixth overall by Boston in 1978, passed up playing in the pros to finish his career at Indiana State, with the complete backing of Auerbach.

"I had never met Bird in my life, but I sure had seen enough of him on TV to know how great he would be as a Celtic," Robey recalls. "I knew he was pretty cocky on the court—and for good reason. I had absolutely no idea what kind of person he was. It sort of amazed me that it took only a couple of weeks for the two of us to become real good friends. We both golfed and we both enjoyed downing some ice cold Millers. Before our first training camp together had ended, we were drinking buddies…. Right off the bat, we'd joke with each other non-stop. I'd kid Larry about being drafted two spots ahead of him in the '78 draft, and he'd come right back and go at me about what he said was the extra four years pro experience I got while playing at Kentucky. It was like we had known each other since we were kids."

In Bird's first year, the Celtics, under their new coach, Bill Fitch, enjoyed the greatest one-year turnaround in NBA history, finishing the regular season with a league-best 61-21 record. Although beaten by Philadelphia, 4-1 in the Eastern Conference finals, Boston clearly was a title contender again. As the backup for both Cowens and Maxwell, Robey was a key contributor. Playing 18 minutes a game, he averaged 11.5 points and 6.5 rebounds while shooting 52 percent from the field. His hard fouls also earned him respect as an intimidator who didn't back down from anyone in the league.

Following their elimination by the Sixers, the Celtics made a major move, acquiring veteran 7-foot-1 center Robert Parish and the third pick of the '80 draft from the Golden State Warriors in exchange for the second and 13th overall selections, which turned out to be heralded center Joe Barry Carroll from Purdue and power forward Rickey Brown from Mississippi State. Boston then chose wide-shouldered, long-armed Kevin McHale, a 6'10" power forward from Minnesota, with the pick it had received from the Warriors.

"I knew Robert was a quality player, a finesse type who had a soft jumper, could rebound and block shots. But the first time I saw him at training camp, I thought he looked kind of awkward, I found out differently real quickly," Robey says. "After just one practice, though, I knew exactly how much this McHale kid was going to help. He was smart, had all sorts of moves around the basket, and could defend against Robert, me, and Larry with no problem."

The 1980-'81 season turned out to be the highlight of Robey's career. "I played mostly backup center," he says. "Fitch wanted me to play physically, to lean on guys like Daryl Dawkins, Wes Unseld, and Bill Cartwright, all the big horses in the league. My job was to soften them up a little, wear them out so Robert could run them into the ground. For me, that was fun.

"With Kevin, Larry, and Max rotating at the forward spots and Robert sprinting up and down the court, we'd get out to a big lead, and teams would just give up. They'd surrender by halftime. It was like we were messing with their minds, especially with Larry and Kevin talking trash all the time."

Boston won 62 games in the regular season but had to sweat out a draining seven-game playoff series against Philly to reach the NBA finals, nipping the 76ers, 91-90, in the deciding game at Boston Garden.

In the NBA title series, the Celtics faced Houston and its inside force, Moses Malone, the league's best and most ferocious rebounder. "He was an animal, a beast," says Robey. "All Fitch told me before the first game was to do whatever was necessary to keep Malone away from the basket. 'I need to give me at least 15 strong minutes. Push him, bump him, shove him, elbow him, tackle him. Just don't let him get inside position on you,' Bill told me. 'And one more thing: Don't foul out.'

"I didn't, either. We beat them in six games, and I must have picked up 24 [actually 21] personals in the series. I remember Robert kidding me by calling me 'The Butcher.' I didn't mind Chief's new nickname for me because I could see that Malone was getting frustrated. There were a couple of times when I hacked him so hard that I swear he was close to slugging me. I loved the war I had with Moses because I realized that's what Fitch wanted from me."

Robey would play two more seasons with Boston. "My minutes went way down because Fitch and then K. C. Jones, who replaced Bill as head coach in 1982, were using McHale to play not only power forward but also to back up Robert at center. By the end of the 1982-'83 season, I saw the handwriting on the wall," he says. "K. C., who not only was my coach but also was a great friend, called me to let me know I was being traded to Phoenix for DJ. I think K. C. expected me to be upset, but I wasn't. I just told him, 'Look, I'd make that deal myself. You're getting the league's best defensive guard.'"

As a Sun, Robey went through three years of torture due to a series of injuries. "I would have gotten a chance to start and play a lot of minutes," he says. "From the beginning, though, I suffered one injury after another. I had a bum knee my first year. I only played four games my second season there because of chronic pain in my right Achilles tendon. Finally, my hip went. I literally couldn't walk. At the end of the 1985-'86 season, I retired."

Despite the ailments, Robey, who underwent a total hip replacement in 1994, has no regrets about sitting on the Phoenix bench as a mere spectator. "The Suns were great to me," he says. "I have no complaints at all. Things just didn't work out the way I wanted."

In 1987, Robey opened a restaurant in Lexington, Kentucky. "The food was excellent, and we were packing the place. The first six months were very successful," he says. "Then it became obvious that money was disappearing. I was so disappointed in certain people I trusted that I decided to just close the doors for good."

Moving to Louisville, he became a licensed real estate agent. "I was fortunate to learn a great deal about the business from two great partners," he says. "We opened up a RE/MAX firm in the region, which includes all of Kentucky. Today were ranked 41st of all the Re/MAX offices in the entire country." Among Robey's clients are horse trainer D. Wayne Lukas and former Celtics coach Rick Pitino. "They're good friends of mine," he says. "Wayne and I owned a horse together, and we might buy a couple more."

He and his wife, Bonnie, have also purchased a medical device sales company, which sells five different types of back braces to orthopedic specialists and their clients, as well as hospitals and physical rehab centers. "We have five territories throughout the South and we're planning on expanding up the East Coast," he says. "They're all profitable and growing."

In his spare time, Robey travels on the weekends to watch his son, Sam, a 6'5", 310-pound center, start for the University of Florida football team. "He has another year of eligibility, so naturally he's hoping to get a shot of playing in the NFL."